Government Failure:
E. G. West on Education

Government Failure:
E. G. West on Education

EDITED BY JAMES TOOLEY &
JAMES STANFIELD

FOREWORD BY ANTONY JAY

The Institute of Economic Affairs

First published in Great Britain in 2003 by
The Institute of Economic Affairs
2 Lord North Street
Westminster
London SW1P 3LB
in association with Profile Books Ltd

The mission of the Institute of Economic Affairs is to improve public understanding of the fundamental institutions of a free society, with particular reference to the role of markets in solving economic and social problems.

A CIP catalogue record for this book is available from the British Library.

ISBN 0 255 36552 7

Many IEA publications are translated into languages other than English or are reprinted. Permission to translate or to reprint should be sought from the Director General at the address above.

Typeset in Stone by MacGuru Ltd
info@macguru.org.uk

Printed and bound in Great Britain by Hobbs the Printers

CONTENTS

THE EDITORS

James Tooley

James Tooley is Professor of Education Policy and Director of the E. G. West Centre at the University of Newcastle upon Tyne. In 1998, he directed the International Finance Corporation's global study of private education and has authored several publications, including *Education without the State, The Global Education Industry, Reclaiming Education* and *The Miseducation of Women*. James Tooley is currently directing a two-year research programme examining how the private sector can satisfy the educational needs of the poor in developing countries, including India, China, Kenya, Ghana and Nigeria. He gained his PhD from the Institute of Education, University of London, in 1994, and has held research positions at the universities of Oxford and Manchester and the National Foundation for Educational Research.

James Stanfield

James Stanfield graduated in business studies in 1994 and is currently a PhD student at the E. G. West Centre, University of Newcastle upon Tyne. His research programme challenges the concept of free and compulsory state schooling as a human right and examines the importance of positive pricing in education, especially within developing countries. He is co-author with James Tooley and Pauline Dixon of *Delivering Better Education: Market Solutions for Educational Improvement*, published by the Adam Smith Institute in June 2003, and also edits the E. G. West Centre's website (www.ncl.ac.uk/egwest).

FOREWORD

Yes Minister and *Yes Prime Minister* were never intended to preach a political or economic doctrine. The founding perception was that there was a wide gap between the rhetoric of democratic government and the realities of actually running a country, and that the gap was rich in comic potential. Our purpose was to expose and exploit that potential in order to entertain audiences, not to reform society. Nevertheless, I cannot pretend that my contacts with the Institute of Economic Affairs did not help me see many more aspects of the comedy of bureaucrats' and politicians' attempts to defend the indefensible.

One of the most hilarious absurdities was education. The system rested on the denial of choice to all parents except the wealthy. Those who deplored this inequality sought to remove it not by extending choice to the less well-off but by denying it to the better-off as well. The defence of the system rested on the absurd argument that politicians, educationists and officials know better than parents what education our children need unless they are in the top income bracket. The argument absolutely demanded a place in our comedy series.

That particular episode, part of the script of which appears as the epilogue to Occasional Paper 130, obviously owes a great deal to the writings of E. G. West, which were almost sacred texts at the IEA. In particular, his demonstration of the high levels of literacy before education was made compulsory blew the arguments for the status quo out of the water. I was also much attracted to the idea of educational vouchers, so vigorously championed by Arthur and Marjorie Seldon. It is arguable that the state has no business financing education at all, but if it does, then everything learnt at the IEA shows that the fatal error is to subsidise the producer and not the consumer. Giving government money to schools not only takes all effective choice away from citizens, it also creates a massive bureaucratic superstructure of inspectors, auditors, committee advisers and administrators, with an accompanying blizzard of regulations, guidelines, consultative documents, reports and instructions which practically bring the cost of educating a child up to the levels of good private schools, which manage without these bureaucratic luxuries. By contrast, giving the money to parents restores their choice and creates competition between schools – competition that is far more effective in raising standards than bureaucratic control and regulatory frameworks.

At the time of writing there does not seem to be much hope of education being returned to the people, but if (dare I say 'when'?) it is, E. G. West will take more credit than anyone else. His writings, some of which are contained in Occasional Paper 130, deserve to be influential and to be taken seriously by anybody studying or working in the field of education or education policy today.

SIR ANTONY JAY

Co-author, Yes Minister *and* Yes Prime Minister

ACKNOWLEDGEMENTS

This book has been made possible by the generosity of Ann West, who donated her late husband's library and papers to the E. G. West Centre (www.ncl.ac.uk/egwest), University of Newcastle upon Tyne, in June 2002. For that we shall be forever grateful.

SUMMARY

- Before government compulsion and widespread government provision of education, private provision was widespread – even among the poor.
- Only a very small minority of parents cannot be trusted to choose their education for their children. Compulsory, uniform provision is not an appropriate way to deal with that problem.
- The portrayal in English literature of nineteenth-century private education in Britain has no basis in fact.
- The proponents of compulsory state-provided education at the time of its origin generally believed that state provision was important to help form the thinking of the young and to prevent them from entering a criminal lifestyle. The first of these objectives is suspect in principle; there is no evidence to suggest that the second has been achieved in practice.
- If the objective of state involvement in education is to ensure that the less well-off have access to education, this should be achieved by government schemes to fund parents, not by making universal, compulsory provision.
- There is huge opposition to school choice within the establishment of the current education system.
- Voucher schemes are both desirable and feasible and are of the greatest benefit to the poor; indeed, voucher schemes can

be specially directed at aiding access to education by the poor.

- A voucher system allows greater choice, provides incentives to schools and ensures that the information contained in price signals is communicated to the providers of education so they use scarce resources to meet the diverse needs of parents, families and children.
- A genuine market in education would lead to the development of new ways of providing education that we cannot, at the present time, even envisage.

TABLES

**Government Failure:
E. G. West on Education**

1   INTRODUCTION
James Tooley

West's challenge

I first came across the writings of Edwin G. West in 1989. As a graduate student at the University of London, I was working on a thesis in philosophy of education. I set out to oppose moves towards 'markets' and 'privatisation' in education, motivated by Thatcherite reforms that were worrying the political 'left' (of which I counted myself a paid-up member) at the time. Scanning the shelves in the old library of the Institute of Education, I came across *Education and the State*.[1] It was an old copy that had not apparently been borrowed for some time. It certainly wasn't on any reading list of courses I was attending, nor recommended to me by my PhD supervisor, nor by anyone else working at the Institute. When I browsed through its contents, and then settled down to read, I wondered why on earth not.

For the book set out a truly revolutionary thesis. It threatened to challenge everything I believed in about education. For me, the fact that governments rightfully intervened in education was a taken-for-granted norm – so taken for granted that it didn't really come up in discussion. I shared this belief with practically everyone else I knew working in the field. Any deviation from

1   E. G. West, *Education and the State*, IEA, London, 1965.

the status quo – such as moves towards markets in education – needed to be justified, not state intervention itself. E. G. West's argument threatened to completely overturn this cosy presumption. For West argued that, prior to the major state involvement in education in England & Wales in 1870, school attendance rates and literacy rates were well above 90 per cent. State intervention was not required to ensure almost universal attendance and literacy. When government got involved with education, it was 'as if it jumped into the saddle of a horse that was already galloping'.[2] Worse still: state involvement crowded out all the private provision that was catering very well for the educational needs of the poor and in the process wrested control and responsibility away from parents.

If West was right, then the significance of his argument stood out in stark relief: for it threw the onus of proof right back on to those who wanted to support government intervention, not on those, like the market reformers, who wanted to move away from it. If, historically, the poor managed without the state, and government intervention eliminated their cost-effective means of gaining education, undermining their control and responsibility for it, then there could be no easy acceptance of the statist status quo. If West was right ... but of course, West must be wrong: or so I thought. My thesis became focused on showing why he was misguided. For a philosopher of education, there was plenty of room to challenge his argument, exploring in much more detail than West had done concepts such as equality, social justice, democracy and public goods, concepts that would show why we needed state intervention in education. Far from proving him

2   Ibid, p. 173.

wrong, however, I eventually had to conclude that he was in all relevant respects correct.

West's work changed the direction of my studies, and the course of my work, as I progressed from my thesis to the study and practice of how the private sector could play a greater role in education, particularly in developing countries. I am in good company: Nobel laureate Milton Friedman wrote to E. G. West: 'I am only one of many who has had his views changed by your path-breaking work. We want more!'[3] Indeed, in the 1980 book Friedman wrote with his wife Rose, *Free to Choose*,[4] they make it clear how they changed their minds about government compulsion and funding on examining the works of E. G. West.

The influence of West on policy

Indeed, it is safe to say that *Education and the State* (now in its third edition), together with numerous articles on the economics of education, public choice and the history of economic thought, and West's second major book, *Education and the Industrial Revolution* (1975, reprinted in 2001 by Liberty Fund), have had an important behind-the-scenes influence on current reforms on privatisation and public–private partnerships in education, both in the UK, the USA and in developing countries. In the UK, West's ideas were carried forward by scholars working at the IEA in particular, and were influential during the Thatcher years on school reform involving parental choice, local management, devolved budgets and the undermining of the power

---

3   On the award of the first Alexis de Tocqueville Award for the Advancement of Education Freedom.

4   Harcourt Brace Jovanovich, New York, 1980, p. 162 and fn 15.

of the local education authorities. Similarly, in the USA and Canada, he has been influential on numerous scholars working in the area of school choice and competition. West's first book, says Washington scholar Dr Myron Lieberman, 'is the single most outstanding intellectual challenge to public education. It is the book the proponents of state-run education must refute or concede the argument.'

Internationally, moreover, E. G. West was commissioned to write two important papers by the World Bank.[5] These explored the role of government and market solutions to education in a variety of developed and developing country contexts – and demonstrated the global significance of his ideas and work. Following this, E. G. West was a leading figure on the team that was commissioned by the International Finance Corporation (IFC – the private finance arm of the World Bank) to explore amongst other things the role of private education in promoting equitable development in developing countries. The report, investigating private education in a dozen developing countries, was submitted in 1998, and led to the IFC and World Bank revising their education policy to favour a greater role for the private sector.

So West's influence has been great – even if his ideas were not acknowledged on any reading list at the London Institute of Education. For his 80th birthday celebrations in February 2002, we invited him to present a lecture in Newcastle upon Tyne – where he wrote *Education and the State* – and to take part in a celebratory dinner at the IEA in London. A few months before, however, in October 2001, he died after a long battle with cancer. This book is

---

5   *Education with and without the State*, World Bank, HCO Working Paper 61, 1995, and *Education Vouchers in Practice and Principle: a world survey*, World Bank, HCO Working Paper 64, 1996, reprinted as Chapter 9 below.

to mark our appreciation of him as a man and as a scholar, and to help others become aware of his ideas, to carry forward his influence.

E. G. West ruffling feathers

Education and the State provoked a sharply polarised debate at the time of its publication. *The Teacher*, on the one hand, described it as a 'polemic' written from 'Dr West's stagnant little academic backwater' (2 November 1965). The *Times Literary Supplement* said that West gave the 'impression of an ill-tempered Chesterton on an off-night … Mr West has asked the wrong questions' (27 January 1966). The *Local Government Chronicle* held that 'Dr West and his colleagues have turned up an academic *cul de sac*', with a book that held not the 'slightest relevance to educational finance' (20 November 1965).

On the other hand, the *Sunday Times* described *Education and the State* as 'perhaps the most important work written on the subject this century'. It continued, 'Dr West, by turning orthodox doctrine inside out, has effected a Copernican revolution' (21 November 1965). Perhaps surprisingly, the *Times Educational Supplement* supported this line, judging that 'Few books more worth serious attention by educationists have come out in the last few years.' *Education and the State*, it suggested, was a 'remarkably able and lively critique of the system and principles under which education is provided by the state … Dr West is one of those rare and invigorating spirits who ask us to glance freshly at what we take for granted and then consider whether it is defensible' (quoted in the *New Statesman*, 10 December 1965: 925).

Nor was the discussion confined to developed countries. The

Economic Times of India, Bombay edition, argued that *Education and the State* 'deserves to be read … it is undoubtedly worthwhile for policy-makers, even in the socialistic political culture of India, to be aware of a line of argument which undoubtedly stems from a totally different historical situation' (31 January 1966). Another reviewer[6] noted, 'At a time when the private sector in education in India is threatened with extinction … Dr West furnishes a power-ful armoury of arguments against Statism in education. Condi-tions in India differ radically from those in England, but to us as to those in that distant island the same choice between freedom and totalitarianism in education has been presented.'

But it was a review in the *New Statesman*, in extraordinarily intemperate language, by Dr (now Professor Emeritus) A. H. ('Chelly') Halsey, of Nuffield College, Oxford, which illustrates most profoundly how the ideas upset the prevailing intellectual climate: 'Of all the verbal rubbish scattered about by the Institute of Economic Affairs,' Halsey begun, 'this book is so far the most pernicious.' 'Mr West's ideas', he wrote, 'are a crass and dreary imitation of those published several years ago by Professor Milton Friedman – a man whose brilliance in argument is made futile by the absurd irrelevance of his 19th century assumptions.' 'Mr West', said Halsey, 'is a man who knows nothing about psychology, soci-ology, and who has less understanding of economics than first year students'; as for history: 'When it comes to the history of educa-tion in the 19th century, Mr West goes beyond tolerable error.' Philosophically, his discussion of 'equality of opportunity' was 'hopeless'. Far from being an 'impartial enquiry', West had writ-

---

6   In a book review section of an Indian source that we have been unable to trace, found in E. G. West's papers after his death.

ten, Halsey opined, 'a gross distortion of the role of the state in education'. The final nail in the coffin, as far as Halsey was concerned, was that West was far from being 'civilised ... like J. S. Mill'.

As it happened, that review was not the end of the matter for the *New Statesman*. A sober piece in the *Daily Telegraph* of 27 July 1966 reports the outcome:

> Yesterday, after a statement in open court, an unusual action, involving two leading academics, was ended with an apology and costs from the *New Statesman* to the Institute of Economic Affairs.
>
> The Institute last year published a book by Dr Edward [*sic*] West ... Its theme was less State and more parental influence in education.
>
> In the *New Statesman* Dr Halsey, Head of the Department of Social and Administrative Studies at Oxford, violently criticised the book, Dr West and the Institute. The Institute held that the attack went beyond the limits of fair criticism.
>
> So the *New Statesman* has apologised handsomely and paid costs. It is consoling that the wider future of education can generate such heat in the Senior Common Room.

In the High Court on 26 July 1966, the magazine gave an unreserved apology for its 'unjustified attack' on Dr West and the IEA. Its review, it said, gave a totally misleading impression of West's argument. The *New Statesman* published an apology in its edition of 22 July 1966.

Government failure

After E. G. West's death in 2001, several of us who have been influenced by his writings wanted to create a book that would mark our appreciation of his work, and introduce it to a new range of students and interested laypersons – both in the developed and the developing world. We decided to republish a selection of his writings that captured the importance and contemporary relevance of his ideas, which had either never previously been published, or were published in journals that were not accessible to a wider audience. From West's large corpus of work, we decided to narrow things down in four ways. First, to make the volume as accessible as possible, we decided to avoid any of the more technical, mathematical papers – many of which appeared in West's later work on the economics of education. The essays here can be seen as non-technical tasters to the deeper arguments contained elsewhere. Second, West's writings cover a large range of topics in economics and he is well known as an authority on Adam Smith. However, this book focuses only on his writings on education. It was also decided to focus only on the areas of primary and secondary education – for West has also written extensively on 'higher' education, and the arguments on that subject could provide enough material for a companion volume. Finally, we did not want simply to replicate *Education and the State* and his later book, *Education and the Industrial Revolution*, both of which have had new editions published by Liberty Fund in the last ten years. We have provided depth and extension to the arguments used in such works, rather than simply repeating what is contained in those books.

What are the major arguments of West that we believe are especially relevant today? The essays collected here convey five:

- Historically, the educational needs of almost everyone, including the poor, were met without the state, in England & Wales, the USA and elsewhere (Chapter 2)

- The demand for imposing state education was made by important opinion-formers acting on misplaced reasoning and spurious evidence (Chapters 3 and 4)
- In particular, these opinion-formers thought that they could use the machinery of government to impose their educational ideals – but government intervention is not benign in the ways they had supposed (Chapters 5–7)
- There are practical ways in which education can be reclaimed from the state, with examples from all over the world – and interesting historical agitation for some of these reforms (Chapters 8 and 9)
- But if education is reclaimed from the state, then we are also liberated to decouple education and schooling (Chapter 10).

The first West essay (Chapter 2), 'The Spread of Education before Compulsion', briefly outlines the historical argument using experience in England & Wales and New York State. This paper succinctly spells out the major thrust of West's historical argument, and the direction it was to move in. In particular, he argues that 'the author of the famous 1870 Act, W. E. Forster', sought only to 'fill the gaps' left by burgeoning private education, not to replace it. His officials, however, 'were overambitious', creating board schools that were 'often found to have much surplus capacity'. This led inevitably to the lowering of tuition fees, and the resulting 'unfair competition' led to the decline of private schools. Anyone who is unfamiliar with West's historical arguments should be able to read this and come away knowing what is in store.

The second and third essays (Chapters 3 and 4) then outline some of West's powerful critique of important opinion-formers of the eighteenth and nineteenth centuries. First, in a previously

unpublished article, West takes to task the view of private education that Charles Dickens popularised, which still influences the
popular imagination today as the only possible view of education
without the state. However, far from being a typical portrayal of
private education in Victorian England, West points to evidence,
some of it contemporaneous, to show that the infamous 'Dotheboys Hall' of *Nicholas Nickleby* was not representative at all of the
private education on offer at the time. Dickens, says West, 'should
have considered carefully how he himself had become literate,
despite his humble family circumstances'. Instead, West argues,
Dickens was agitating for state education, and used his fiction as a
vehicle to move forward that political agenda.

Charles Dickens, of course, was not alone amongst influential
opinion-formers in wanting state education – although thinkers
were by no means uniformly in favour. The challenge to John
Stuart Mill's views was outlined in 'Liberty and Education: John
Stuart Mill's Dilemma'. The essay first outlines how William Godwin defended the case for negative liberty in education: 'the only
true education was self-education'; for Godwin, 'governments
were corrupt ... and provided only too easy a channel for thinkers
who were arrogant enough to believe that they had the monopoly
of the truth and that their doctrines alone were worthy of forced
consumption through the agency of the state'. Later, John Stuart
Mill, perhaps one of the most influential of all nineteenth-century
liberal thinkers on education, was inconsistent in his treatment
of liberty when it came to education and the role of government.
Yes, on the one hand there is his famous dictum that 'a general
state education is a mere contrivance for moulding people to be
exactly like one another'; but on the other is his argument that
laissez-faire principles completely break down when applied to

children and education, and that a 'well intentioned' government ought to be able to offer 'better education and better instruction to the people' than they could arrange for themselves. Rather than allowing working-class parents to be responsible for the education of their children, a benign state must take away that responsibility for their own good.

But can the state work in this benign fashion? Much of West's later work is focused on the 'economics of politics' (or public choice economics, as it became known), questioning the common assumption that 'political man pursued, not his own, but the public interest'. Under this assumption, he writes, 'progress consists simply in persuading some government to accept reforming ideas' – such as those of the nineteenth-century opinion-formers seeking state intervention. But such an easy assumption is no longer tenable: 'benevolent government does not exist. The political machinery is …, in fact, largely … operated by interest groups, vote-maximising politicians and self-seeking bureaucracies'.[7] Indeed, thinking that it is possible to have such a government is based on a misunderstanding of Adam Smith's 'invisible hand'. In fact, contends West, Adam Smith had in effect *two* 'invisible hands'. The first was the conventional one, where an individual, who 'intends only his own gain', is led by an invisible hand to promote an end that was no part of his intention. But the second invisible hand can be summarised in parallel terms: 'an individual who intends only to serve the public interests by fostering government intervention is led by an invisible hand to promote private interests which was no part of his intention … It was the decline of the recognition of the

---

7   E. G. West, 'The Benthamites as Educational Engineers: The Reputation and the Record', *History of Political Economy* 24(3), 1992, pp. 595–621.

second (rent-seeking) invisible hand that surely accounted, more than anything else, for the increasing nineteenth-century classical departures from Smith's prescription of minimal government.'[8]

Three essays in this collection (Chapters 5 to 7) illustrate some of West's arguments along these lines, addressing issues of supreme contemporary importance, including compulsory schooling and the relationship between state education and juvenile crime.

In 'The Economics of Compulsion', West addresses the paradox that 'Other things being equal, compulsion is more "profitable" to the government the smaller the minority to be compelled. Yet the needs of the children of a small minority of "irresponsible" parents may be met more efficiently if the paternalistic powers of government were concentrated on them, and not diffused over the wide areas where they are not needed.' Universal compulsion, he argues, 'will have indirect costs that are so severe as to outweigh the benefits'. One of these indirect costs concerns crime and juvenile delinquency. In 'Education and Crime: A Political Economy of Interdependence', West examines the question, both historically and in a contemporary setting, of whether or not state education actually reduces crime, as its proponents had historically argued that it would. The contemporary evidence, and its contrast with historical ambitions, doesn't augur well: 'The nineteenth-century Utilitarians planned for a school where children were systematically controlled and instructed in an orderly environment so that when they were old enough to leave they would be a help instead of a menace to society. The most striking modern fact in this context is that the crime and violence the Utilitarians wanted to subdue (and exclude) has now entered the very portals of the

---

8   E. G. West, *Adam Smith and Modern Economics*, Edward Elgar, Aldershot, 1990, p.194.

public school[9] itself.' The risk of violence to teenagers 'is greater in schools than elsewhere'. Such has been one of the unforeseen consequences of state involvement in education.

In 'Public Education and Imperfect Democracy', West explores the paradox of free societies tolerating the existence of 'a coercive education system'. He shows how a favourite attempt to rationalise state education has focused on its role 'as a crucial component of democracy', as giving 'unique protection to the children of the poor'. However, by contrast, West points to conundrums such as the way in which the poor are prevented from escaping ghetto schools, while the middle classes are able to 'buy a house, buy a school'. It is interest groups such as the teaching unions, he suggests, which lead to '*obstacles* to democracy', rather than its encouragement.

If all that West writes is correct, then what is to be done? Essays seven and eight (Chapters 8 and 9) look at West's theoretical and practical research on a range of 'Market Solutions in Education'. Significantly, in 'Tom Paine's Voucher Scheme for Public Education', West shows how the idea for educational vouchers and tax credits can be traced back not to economists such as Milton Friedman, as is commonly argued, but to the social reformer Thomas Paine, in *The Rights of Man*. Next, there is an extensive review that West conducted for the World Bank on vouchers, looking first at their theory, and then the practice from a variety of countries. Interestingly, he outlines voucher policies that have been implemented in countries such as Bangladesh, Chile, Colombia and Lesotho, as well as the USA. In all these countries, vouchers have been seen as vehicles to help promote educational equity and to assist the poor – aims with which West was concerned throughout his career.

9   By 'public' schools, West means state, not private, schools. This US use of the term 'public' school is common throughout this monograph.

The final short essay by West, 'Education without the State', published in 1994, provides a summary of many of West's ideas and practical proposals, useful in conclusion to bring some of the major ideas together. In the end, West's position leads to something even more radical than the educational voucher. His ideas imply the decoupling of the conflation that often occurs between 'education' and 'schooling' – for it is the former, not the latter, which is of greatest importance. In Victorian England, before state intervention, West argues, there was a whole variety of educational inputs into working people's lives, over and above that which they got from school. These include: the 'adult education movement, the mutual improvement societies, the literary and philosophical institutes, the mechanics' institutes, … the Owenite halls of science' and 'freelance lecturers who travelled the towns and stimulated self-study among the poor', as well as the Sunday schools. This 'fluid, flexible, heterogeneous and competitive educational scenario of the pre-1870s' is what we should be looking for in educational reform today. He examines the implication that the 'choice of school movement … has been to a large extent misinformed. What is needed is choice in *education*. School choice has not and will not lead to more productive education because the obsolete technology called "school" is inherently *inelastic*. As long as "school" refers to the traditional structure of buildings and grounds with services delivered in boxes called classrooms to which customers must be transported by car or bus, "school choice" will be unable to meaningfully alter the quality or efficiency of education.' For West argues that 'Genuinely free markets are unpredictable in their unfolding school organisations as well as in their offerings of completely new curricula with which they constantly surprise us.' Pre-1870, there was the basis for 'a truly dynamic and innovative *education* market ... It is unfortunate that this market was destroyed by the combined action of politicians, bureaucrats and rent-seekers.'

West's final thesis is truly radical, as I realised when I first encountered it. Not only does it lead us to question the role of government in education, it also leads us inevitably to question the current conflation of schooling with education, and asks us to contemplate the reclaiming of education – not just from the state but also from schooling.

To conclude the volume, the Epilogue features an extract from the BBC series *Yes Prime Minister*. Sir Antony Jay, the co-author of *Yes Prime Minister*, has told us how he was inspired by the work of E. G. West in his treatment of education, so it seemed a fitting conclusion to the work. Here the fictional mandarin Sir Humphrey is presented with the (equally fictitious) prime minister's radical proposal to sort out state education: give parents choice of schools. Sir Humphrey doesn't like that at all, and points out that neither will the Department for Education. The prime minister's solution would have gladdened the heart of Professor E. G. West: 'We'll abolish it,' he says.

We show in this volume that West's influence is profound and enduring and that it deserves attention, especially now, in this country and globally, as much as, or more so, than it did during his lifetime. Returning to the press cuttings from the time of first publication of West's work, we see that the *Times Educational Supplement* challenged: 'If working-class parents were prepared to back the choice they then possessed with money, *why should they be presumed unfit to choose today when they are so much richer?*' This is the key question that West's work poses for us. It is as relevant today as it was when West was first writing.

2 THE SPREAD OF EDUCATION BEFORE COMPULSION: BRITAIN AND AMERICA IN THE NINETEENTH CENTURY

E. G. West[1]

Most persons agree that children need the protection of the law against potential abuse by parents. But evidence shows that only a small minority of parents turn out to be delinquent. In practice it is very seldom indeed that governments remove children from their family home. At the end of the 1980s fewer than two children per ten thousand below the age of eighteen were under state care in the USA or in England & Wales. That is less than two-hundredths of 1 per cent! (Becker & Murphy, 1988: 3 and fn 9).

It can thus reasonably be assumed that the vast majority of parents are altruistic towards their children, so that, for instance, they will not neglect their food, clothing or shelter. Yet if these necessities were to be provided today on the same basis as education they would be available free of charge. Indeed, there would be laws for compulsory and universal eating and higher taxes to pay for children's 'free' food at the nearest local authority kitchens or shops.

But it is only in the last century and a quarter that this kind of asymmetry of treatment has emerged. This essay will accordingly look at the history of the subject to enquire to what extent the al-

---

1   This essay originally appeared in the *Freeman: Ideas on Liberty* 46(7), July 1996, and is reprinted by kind permission of the Foundation for Economic Education.

truism of typical parents extended to education as well as to other necessities before governments intervened. I shall first examine conditions in England in the nineteenth century prior to the introduction of compulsory education. I shall then make a similar investigation of the USA to see if there were interesting parallels.

England & Wales

Contrary to popular belief, although prior to any government intervention schooling in Britain depended almost completely on private funds between 1800 and 1840, the supply of it was relatively substantial. At this time, moreover, the largest contributors to education revenues were working parents (West, 1975) and the second largest was the Church. Of course, there was less education per child than today, just as there was less of everything else, because the national income was so much smaller. I have calculated, nevertheless, that the percentage of the net national income spent on day schooling of children of all ages in England in 1833 was approximately 1 per cent. By 1920, when schooling had become 'free' and compulsory by special statute, the proportion had fallen to 0.7 per cent (West, 1975: 89).

The evidence also shows that working parents were purchasing increasing amounts of education for their children as their incomes were rising from 1818 onwards, and this, to repeat, at a time before education was 'free' and compulsory by statute. Compulsion came in 1880 and state schooling did not become free until 1891.

Table 1 demonstrates that the annual growth of enrolments between 1818 and 1858 exceeded the annual growth of population. After the compilation of the first educational census in 1851, it was

Table 1   **Growth in public schooling in England & Wales, 1818–58**

Year	Population	Average annual growth rate of population	No. of day scholars	Average annual growth rate of day scholars
1818	11,642,683		674,883	
		1.40%		3.60%
1833	14,386,415		1,276,947	
		1.47%		3.16%
1851	17,927,609		2,144,378	
		1.21%		2.35%
1858	19,523,103		2,525,462	

Sources: 1851 Census (Education Report) and the Newcastle Commission Report on Education in 1858 (Parliamentary Papers, 1861).

reported that the average school attendance period of working-class children was nearly five years. By 1858 the Newcastle Commission concluded that it had risen to nearly six years. And the same authority reported that 'almost every one receives some amount of school education at some period or other' (Newcastle Commission, 1861: 293).

The author of the famous 1870 Act, W. E. Forster, explained that the intention of introducing fee-paying government-run establishments for the first time was not to replace the vast system of private schools but simply to 'fill up the gaps' where they could be found. His officials, however, were overambitious in their reports of these needs, and after government schools were erected they were often found to have much surplus capacity. To reduce their embarrassment over half-empty schools, the education boards then resorted to lowering tuition fees and using tax revenues to fill the breach. The lower price naturally expanded the demand; but this was at the expense of the private schools, many of which could not survive such unfair competition.

After education was made compulsory by statute, the government school advocates argued that it was wrong to compel the very poorest to do something they could not afford. But rather than propose a special financial dispensation or grants to these families, the advocates insisted that education should be made free for all: the rich and the middle class as well as the lower-income groups. Free education was legislated for the new government schools exclusively because it was argued that it would be inviting conflict to ask taxpayers to subsidise religious schools. Protestant taxpayers, for instance, would object to their taxes financing Catholics, and vice versa.

In this way the new 'gap-filling' government schools were given a wide-open field with their zero-priced education. Since most of the subsequent growing population naturally chose the 'free' alternative, the private schools' share of the market declined and that of government schools sky-rocketed.

The literacy record

The pre-1870 record of educational outputs such as literacy was even more impressive than the numbers of children in school, and this presents an even more serious problem to typical authors of social histories. Professor Mark Blaug (1975: 595) has observed that 'Conventional histories of education neatly dispose of the problem by simply ignoring the literacy evidence.'

R. K. Webb, a specialist historian of literacy, offers the following conclusions about conditions in Britain in the late 1830s: 'in so far as one dare generalize about a national average in an extraordinarily varied situation, the figure would seem to run between two-thirds and three-quarters of the working classes as literate, a group which included most of the respectable poor who were the great political potential in English life'.[2]

There was, moreover, an appreciable rate of *growth* in literacy. This is reflected in the fact that young persons were more and more accomplished than their elders. Thus a return of the educational requirements of men in the navy and marines in 1865 showed that 99 per cent of the boys could read compared with seamen (89 per cent), marines (80 per cent) and petty officers (94 per cent).[3]

It is not surprising that with such evidence of literacy growth among young people, the levels had become even more substantial by 1870. On my calculations (West, 1978), in 1880, when national compulsion was enacted, over 95 per cent of fifteen-year-olds were literate. This should be compared to the fact that over a century later 40 per cent of 21-year-olds in the UK admit to difficulties with writing and spelling (Central Statistical Office, 1995: 58).

American education on the eve of government compulsion

In the interests of manageability I shall confine attention to a single US state. New York is selected because it seems to have been reasonably representative of conditions generally in the first 70 years of nineteenth-century America. In 1811 five commissioners were authorised to report on the extent of education in the state. They recognised that, in order to qualify for state aid, it was necessary to establish in what respects the people were not themselves already securing sufficient education for their children. The commissioners

---

2   Webb, 1963: 149.
3   Ibid.

acknowledged that schooling was indeed already widespread: 'In a free government, where political equality is established, and where the road to preferment is open to all, there is a natural stimulus to education; and accordingly *we find it generally resorted to, unless some great local impediments* interfere.'[4]

Poverty was in some cases an impediment; but the biggest obstacle was bad geographic location:

> In populous cities, and the parts of the country thickly settled, *schools are generally established by individual exertion.* In these cases, the means of education are facilitated, as the expenses of schools are divided among a great many. It is in the remote and thinly populated parts of the State, where the inhabitants are scattered over a large extent, that education stands greatly in need of encouragement. The people here living far from each other, makes it difficult so to establish schools as to render them convenient or accessible to all. Every family therefore, must either educate its own children, or the children must forgo the advantages of education.[5]

The problem was thus presented in the same terms as those later used in England by W. E. Forster, the architect of the 1870 English Education Act. As we have seen, it was largely a problem, to use Forster's words, of 'filling up the gaps'. The logic of such argument, of course, called mainly for discriminating and marginal government intervention. To this end three methods were available. First, the government could assist families, but only the needy ones, by way of educational subsidies. Second, it could subsidise the promoters of schools in the special areas where they were needed.

---

4   Randall, 1871: 18 (my emphasis).
5   Ibid. (my emphasis).

Third, the government itself could set up schools, but only in the 'gap' areas. Without discussing possible alternatives, the New York state commissioners recommended that the inconveniences could generally best be remedied 'by the establishment of Common Schools, under the direction and patronage of the State'.

The report, having stressed the plight of the rural areas, leads the reader to expect special attention to be paid to them in the New York State general plan of intervention. No such priority appears, however. The main features of the plan suggested by the commissioners were: that the several towns of the state be divided into school districts by three commissioners, elected by the citizens to vote for town offices; that three trustees be elected in each district, to whom shall be confined the care and superintendence of the school to be established therein; that the interest of the school fund be divided among the different counties and towns, according, not to the distribution, but to the size of their respective populations as ascertained by the current census of the United States.

Thus, in place of discrimination in favour of the poor and thinly populated districts, a flat equality of treatment was decreed for *all areas*; the public monies were to be distributed on a per capita basis according to the number of children between five and fifteen in each district, whether its population was dense or sparse, rich or poor.

Two details of the early legislation (of 1812 and 1814) are worthy of special attention. First, there seems to have been no announced intention of making education free. Even with the addition of the revenues from town taxes there were far from sufficient monies to cover expenses. The substantial balance was presented in the form of rate bills (fees) to the parents, who were required to pay in proportion to the attendance of their children. For instance, in

1830 parental fees contributed $346,807 towards the total sum for teachers' wages of $586,520.[6]

The second detail of the early legislation worth noticing is that religion was regarded as an integral part of school education. The commissioners observed: 'Morality and religion are the foundation of all that is truly great and good; and consequently, of primary importance.'[7] The Bible, in Common Schools, was to be treated as more than a literary work. The commissioners particularly recommended the practice of the New York Free Schools (the charitable establishments) in 'presuming the religious regard which is due to the sacred writings'.[8]

Subsequently the annual reports of the superintendents revealed a steady growth in the number of school districts organised. In some cases, entirely new schools were built; in others the personnel of existing private schools allowed themselves to become socialised – that is, to become Common Schools – in order to qualify for the public monies. In the report of 1821 it was stated that the whole number of children between the ages of five and sixteen residing in the state was 380,000; and the total number of all ages taught during the year was 342,479. Thus, according to this evidence, schooling in the early nineteenth century was already almost universal without being compulsory. Moreover, although it was subsidised, it was not free except to the very poor.

In the first half of the century figures for private schooling throughout the state were hard to come by. But it will be remembered that the 1811 commissioners observed that in thickly populated areas the means of education were already well provided for. The

6   Ibid., p. 66. Teachers' wages constituted about one half of total expenses.

7   Ibid., p. 19.

8   Ibid., p. 22.

superintendents' report of 1830 contained an account of a census of the schools of the city of New York for the year 1829. It showed that of the 24,952 children attending school in the city, the great majority, 18,945, were in private schools.[9]

By this time the superintendents were expressing complete satisfaction with the provision of schooling. On the quantity of it the report of 1836 asserted: 'Under any view of the subject, it is reasonable to believe, that in the Common Schools, private schools and academies, the number of children actually receiving instruction is equal to the whole number between five and sixteen years of age.'[10]

The fact that education could continue to be universal without being free and compulsory seems to have been readily acknowledged. Where there were scholars who had poor parents, the trustees had authority to release them from the payment of fees entirely, and this was done 'at the close of term, in such a manner as to divest the transaction of all the circumstances calculated to wound the feelings of scholars'.[11]

Literacy in nineteenth-century America

The spread of literacy among the American population before education became compulsory seems to have been at least as impressive as in the case of Britain. An item in the *Journal of Education* of January 1828 gave this account:

> Our population is 12,000,000, for the education of which, we have 50 colleges, besides several times the number of

---

9   1830 *Ann. Rep. N.Y. Supt. Common Schools*, p. 17.

10 1836 *Ann. Rep. N.Y. Supt. Common Schools*, p. 8.

11 1831 *Ann. Rep. N.Y. Supt. Common Schools*, p. 16.

well endowed and flourishing academies leaving primary schools out of the account. For meeting the intellectual wants of this 12,000,000, we have about 600 newspapers and periodical journals. There is no country, (it is often said), where the means of intelligence are so generally enjoyed by all ranks and where knowledge is so generally diffused among the lower orders of the community, as in our own. The population of those portions of Poland which have successively fallen under the dominion of Russia, is about 20,000,000. To meet the wants of which there are but 15 newspapers, eight of which are printed in Warsaw. But with us a newspaper is the daily fare of almost every meal in almost every family.

Richman (1994) quotes data showing that from 1650 to 1795 American male literacy climbed from 60 to 90 per cent. Between 1800 and 1840 literacy in the North rose from 75 per cent to between 91 and 97 per cent. In the South the rate grew from about 55 per cent to 81 per cent. Richman also quotes evidence indicating that literacy in Massachusetts was 98 per cent on the eve of legislated compulsion and is about 91 per cent today.

Finally, Carl F. Kaestle (1973) observes: 'The best generalization possible is that New York, like other American towns of the Revolutionary period, had a high literacy rate relative to other places in the world, and that literacy did not depend primarily upon the schools.'

Conclusion

This account of education in New York State prior to full government intervention to make it 'free', compulsory and universal can be concluded as follows. Whether or not it was appropriate (after

1867) to apply compulsion unconditionally to all classes of individuals, the laws that were actually established did not in fact secure an education that was universal in the sense of 100 per cent school attendance by all children of school age. If, on the other hand, the term 'universal' is intended more loosely to mean something like 'most', 'nearly everybody' or 'over 90 per cent', then we lack firm evidence to show that education was not already universal prior to intervention. The eventual establishment, meanwhile, of laws to provide a schooling that was both compulsory and 'free' was accompanied by major increases in costs. These included not only the unprecedented expenses of growing bureaucracy but also the substantial costs of reduced liberty of families eventually caught in a choice-restricted monopoly system serving the interests not of the demanders but of the rent-seeking suppliers. Both sides of the Atlantic shared this fate.

References

Becker, G., and K. Murphy (1988), 'The Family and the State', *Journal of Law and Economics* 30: 1–19.

Blaug, Mark (1975), 'The Economics of Education in English Classical Political Economy: A Re-examination', in A. Skinner and T. Wilson, *Essays on Adam Smith*, Clarendon Press, Oxford.

Central Statistical Office (1995), *Social Trends*, HMSO, London.

Kaestle, Carl F. (1973), *The Evolution of the School System: New York City 1750–1850*, Harvard University Press, Cambridge, MA.

Newcastle Commission (1861), 'The Royal Commission on Popular Education'.

Randall, M. (1871), *History of the Common School System of the State of New York, from Its Origins in 1795, to the Present Time*, Ivison, Blakeman, Taylor, & Co., New York.

Richman, Sheldon (1994), *Separating School and State*, Future of Freedom Foundation, Fairfax, VA.

Webb, R. K. (1963), 'The Victorian Reading Public', in *From Dickens to Hardy*, Pelican Books, Harmondsworth.

West, E. G. (1967), 'The Political Economy of American Public School Legislation', *Journal of Law and Economics* 10: 101–28.

West, E. G. (1975), *Education and the Industrial Revolution*, Batsford, London.

West, E. G. (1978), 'Literacy and the Industrial Revolution', *Economic History Review* 31(3), August.

3 PUBLIC EDUCATION: A DICKENS OF A MESS!

E. G. West[1]

Charles Dickens's continuing influence upon the twentieth-century popular imagination as regards educational conditions in the nineteenth century is curious yet understandable. For many years he has figured in school textbooks as a source of colourful illustrations of early Victorian social history. His entertainment value, meanwhile, is still unsurpassed, while his *Nicholas Nickleby* continues in popularity not only in literature but now also on radio, film and television. Entertainment apart, however, it is curious how Dickens's impressions are used without qualification in specialist works on the history of education.[2] We do not suggest for one moment that Dickens, who, together with his incomparable talents as a novelist, also displayed the zeal of the reformer and the instincts of the newspaper reporter, should be entirely discarded as a contemporary source now that in the twentieth century we have access to new and more efficient types of historiography. What we do propose, however, is some fresh empirical verification and assessment of the Dickens verdict and approach.

Born in 1812, Dickens lived in Chatham until about 1823 and spent the next ten years in London. *Nicholas Nickleby* was first

---

1   Previously unpublished, although a shorter version appeared in *Competition*, newsletter of the Council for a Competitive Economy, USA, April 1980.

2   In his *History of Education in Great Britain* (1965), S. J. Curtis uses Dotheboys Hall as an exemplar of the 'terrible conditions' of the private schools (see p. 234).

published in monthly parts from April 1838 to October 1839, and the novel was first issued in book form in October 1839. In the preface, the author explains that he came to hear about Yorkshire schools when a 'not very robust child'. His first impressions of them (probably through newspaper reports) were 'somehow or other connected with a suppurated abscess that some boy had come home with, in consequence of his Yorkshire guide, philosopher, and friend, having ripped it open with an inky pen-knife'. This story stuck with him ever after and he determined one day to follow it up in a report to the public at large. *Nicholas Nickleby* was commenced within a few months after the publication of the completed *Pickwick Papers*, which must have been in 1837. Dickens insists in his preface that Mr Squeers, the Yorkshire headmaster, and his school 'are faint and feeble pictures of an existing reality, purposely subdued, and kept down lest they should be deemed impossible'. His evidence for his belief that he had under-written rather than over-written his story came from accounts of atrocities committed on neglected children supplied from private quarters far beyond the reach of suspicion or distrust, and from past reporting of trials at law 'in which damages have been sought as a poor recompense for lasting agonies and disfigurements inflicted on children'. He explains that he had resolved, had he seen occasion, 'to reprint a few of these details of legal proceedings from certain old newspapers'. Unfortunately Dickens did not divulge much more about these private sources.

Dickens was obviously previously prepared when he made a personal visit to Yorkshire one very severe winter (probably that of 1837/8). Wishing to avoid notice as the celebrated author of *Pickwick*, he 'concerted a pious fraud' with a professional friend who had a Yorkshire connection. The friend supplied Dickens with letters of introduction in a fictitious name. They referred 'to a supposititious [*sic*] little boy who had been left with a widowed mother who didn't know what to do with him; the poor lady had thought, as a means of thawing the tardy compassion of her relations in his behalf, of sending him to a Yorkshire school; I was the poor lady's friend travelling that way; and if the recipient of the letter could inform me of a school in the neighbourhood, the writer would be very much obliged'. After Dickens had obtained local information in this manner he returned to Kent and completed his book at the age of 25 or 26.

The publication of *Nicholas Nickleby* in 1838 caused considerable indignation among many Yorkshire people, who regarded the story as an unjust indictment.[3] At the same time it prompted public outrage and demands for immediate action in the interests of children. An intensive official survey of the West Riding of Yorkshire in the late 1850s was conducted by J. G. Fitch, the Assistant Commissioner to the Newcastle Commission. He reported: 'I have wholly failed to discover any example of the typical Yorkshire boarding-school with which Dickens' *Nicholas Nickleby* has made us familiar. I have seen schools in which board and education were furnished for £20 and even £18 per annum, but have been unable to find evidence of bad feeding or physical neglect.'[4]

Due regard should be paid to the fact that this government report was made twenty years after the prototype of Dotheboys Hall existed. The public shock associated with the publication of *Nicholas Nickleby* could have caused subsequent closures of the

3 An account of these reactions is contained in Philip Collins, *Dickens and Education*, 1965.

4 *Schools Inquiry Commission* (for 1858), vol. I, 1861, p.32. Fitch's remarks are also quoted in Curtis, op. cit.

worst schools.[5] This indeed is suggested in a preface to a later edition written in 1848. Referring to the fact that the book was written ten years previously, just after *Pickwick*, Dickens observes in retrospect: 'There were, then, a good many cheap Yorkshire schools in existence. There are very few now ... I make mention of the race of Schoolmasters as of the Yorkshire schoolmasters, in the past tense. Although it has not yet finally disappeared, it is dwindling daily.' If Fitch's report cannot strictly be taken to contradict Dickens's view of the 1830s it is still to be considered as an indication of conditions of the 1850s, especially in the light of Dickens's corroborative comments concerning the large number of extinctions by then of bad schools and teachers. It must be borne in mind that private fee-paying schools were still in the 1850s the main agency of education throughout the country.[6]

Whatever the validity of Dickens's account of the early-nineteenth-century schools of the 'Dotheboys' kind, it could never seriously begin to qualify as a representative of private schooling

---

5   In the introduction by Charles Dickens the Younger to an edition of 1892 (Macmillan), there is reference to a story (in the Dickens biography by C. W. Cope) from the driver of a stagecoach between Darlington and Barnard Castle who stated that Dickens ruined a schoolmaster by the name of Shaw, who was alleged to be the prototype of Squeers. The coachman stoutly denied that Squeers's (Shaw's) boys were half starved and explained that Dickens obtained his story from a dismissed usher; 'it was a poisoned source'. Charles Dickens Junior dismissed the idea that an actual prototype of Squeers existed. He also objected to evidence from 'unnamed stage-coachmen and other witnesses of similar nebulosity'. He would have been on stronger ground, however, if the witnesses of Charles Dickens Senior were not similarly 'unnamed'.

6   Those schools that accepted subsidies had also to accept inspection. In this sense there was an element of 'publicness' about them. In the 1851 census they were indeed classified as 'public schools'; but they were still privately owned and continued to charge fees. The main point we wish to emphasise is that they were an entirely different type of organisation from the state schools of today.

in this period – that is, of nearly the whole of early-nineteenth-century English education. The Wackford Squeers establishment was a sample of one particular class of school only: the full board school. The vast majority of schools at this time were day schools. The large quantity of new schools that appeared during the Industrial Revolution made their biggest debut not in the remote parts of the country but in the growing towns. They did so moreover in such numbers as to encourage abundant competition and therefore rapid transit between families and others of daily information about them. The Dickens prototype, moreover, was a subset of its own class. 'Dotheboys Hall' advertised 'No Vacations',[7] suggesting that it was being used purposefully and specially as a place for sending orphans, illegitimates and generally unwanted children from all parts of England, like the 'supposititious [sic] little boy' in Dickens's own letter of introduction.

Despite these observations, Dickens, in his writing, seems to have been speaking for English education as a whole. He did so too in a way that suggested strong Benthamite predilections and overtones. In his later preface to *Nickleby* he wrote: 'Of the monstrous neglect of education in England and the disregard of it by the State as a means of forming good or bad citizens and miserable or happy men, private schools long afforded a notable example.'[8] Dickens made no secret of the fact that his interests in education could in his own times be classed as partisan. His were the views of the contemporary pressure group called the Birmingham League, which favoured compulsory, 'comprehensive', unsectarian and

---

7   Collins, op. cit.

8   Compare this sentence with James Mill's remark that '… the question whether the people should be educated, is the same with the question whether they should be happy or miserable'.

state-provided education; on these issues, Dickens was a ready speaker to popular audiences on the subject.[9]

Whether or not, when he was writing *Nickleby*, the young Dickens had access to the systematic contemporary surveys of schooling made by the statistical societies of Manchester and the other big industrial centres, it is doubtful that he consulted these. Had he done so his grasp of the total educational situation would have been more comprehensive and more in perspective. Yet interestingly enough these same sources would have afforded much colourful and anecdotal material upon which the fertile and creative mind of such a novelist might well have worked.

There is indeed much material in the reporting of the statistical investigators upon the quality of some selected schools which has a considerable and unconscious 'Dickensian' flavour. Most of our quotations will be taken from the report on Manchester in 1834. We should be careful to note, however, that in several respects Manchester was different from other English industrial towns, not least because of a significant proportion of recent Irish immigrants in its population. The fact that over one sixth of the family heads were Irish was partly attributed by the statistical society to the circumstance that Manchester, unlike some other towns, gave relief to the Irish out of the poor rate. Proper study of the Manchester Report serves to illustrate the difficulty of steering a course between a balanced descriptive impression of school conditions (which in a large number of cases were certainly wretched) and a temptation to be carried away by the more lurid, spectacular and 'rumbustious' individual instances. We are sometime apt to

---

9   C. Birchenough, *History of Elementary Education in England and Wales*, 1920, p. 66.

forget that reports written in earnest solemnity often tell us as much about their writers as about their subject. The following is an 'incidental' observation placed in a footnote of the Manchester Statistical Society's Report on Manchester 1834 (p. 10).

> The Committee met with two instances of schools kept by Masters of some abilities, but much given to drinking, who had however gained such a reputation in their neighbourhood, that after spending a week or a fortnight in this pastime they could always fill their schoolrooms again as soon as they returned to their post. The children during the absence of the Masters go to other schools for the week, or play in the streets, or are employed by their parents, in running errands, etc. On another occasion, one of these Instructors and Guardians of the morals of our youth, was met issuing from his school room at the head of his scholars to see a fight in the neighbourhood; and instead of stopping to reply to any educational queries, only uttered a breathless invitation to come along and see the sport.

In another footnote (p. 9) we discover our Manchester investigator coolly attempting to put his questions to a master in a Common School who was simultaneously in charge of a large class and studiously reporting the result as follows:

> In one of these seminaries of learning, where there were about 130 children, the noise and confusion was so great as to render the replies of the Master to the enquiries put to him totally inaudible; he made several attempts to obtain silence but without effect; at length, as a last effort, he ascended his desk, and striking it forcibly with a ruler, said, in a strong Hibernian accent 'I'll tell you what it is, boys, the first I hear make a noise, I'll call him up, and kill entirely!' and then perceiving probably on the countenance of his visitor some expression of dismay at this murderous

threat, he added quickly in a more subdued tone, 'almost I will.' His menace produced no more effect than his previous appeals had done. A dead silence succeeded for a minute or two; then the whispering recommenced, and the talking, shuffling of feet, and general disturbance was soon as bad as ever.

The writer does not make it entirely clear whether all 130 boys were in the same room. If this was so then the case must have been very exceptional, since the Manchester Statistical Society's figures showed an average teacher pupil ratio of 1 to 34 for the 179 Common Schools. (The average ratio for Manchester, Bury, Salford, York, Birmingham and Liverpool was 1 to 26.8.)

The Manchester Dame Schools for children from two years upwards afforded probably some of the most 'Dickensian' examples of all. The contemporary relative poverty showed up here in several aspects. Often mainly acting on child-minding enterprises, the Dame Schools allowed parents the opportunity to earn bigger incomes for the family. This function was combined with rudimentary attempts at instruction, especially in reading and sewing. When assessing these schools it is as well to remember that they contained large numbers below the age of five, an age group for which, even in 1970, the English state system still makes hardly any school provision at all. Many Dame Schools were found in 'dirty' and 'unwholesome' rooms – how much more unwholesome and dirty than the typical dwelling of the time is not discoverable. Certainly, by twentieth-century standards the physical conditions of Manchester were grim. 'In one of these schools eleven children were found, in a small room in which one of the children of the Mistress was lying in bed ill of the measles. Another child had died in the same room of the same complaint a few days before; and no less than thirty of the usual scholars were then confined at home with the same disease.'[10]

School furniture and books were often a luxury: 'In another school all the children to the number of twenty, were squatted upon the bare floor there being no benches, chairs, or furniture of any kind, in the room. The Master said his terms would not yet allow him to provide forms, but he hoped that as his school increased, and his circumstances thereby improved, he should be able sometime or other to afford this luxury.'[11]

Some of the teachers could not make a living wage out of such teaching and had to augment it with other employment, such as shopkeeping, sewing and washing. Of all the graphic footnotes in the Manchester Report for 1834 (p. 6), the following is the most poignant and bizarre: 'One of the best of these schools is kept by a blind man who hears his scholars their lessons, and explains them with great simplicity; he is however liable to interruption in his academic labours, as his wife keeps a mangle, and he is obliged to turn it for her.'

The Birmingham Statistical Society reported that: 'The physical condition of the dame schools of Birmingham is much more satisfactory than could have been anticipated. None of them are kept in cellars, very few in garrets or bedrooms, and they are generally more cleanly and better lighted than schools of the same description in Manchester and Liverpool.'[12]

Forty-four per cent of the Birmingham Dame School scholars were under five years old. Clearly anxious to enquire about the moral and religious aspects of the teaching, the investigators were

10   Manchester Report (p. 6).
11   Ibid.
12   Report for the year 1838, April 1840.

often taken aback by the replies: 'A mistress in one of this class of schools, on being asked whether she gave moral instruction to her scholars, replied, "No, I can't afford it for 3*d* a week."'

Another replied: 'How is it likely, when they can hardly say their A, B, C?'

In only 21 out of 267 schools was 'moral instruction' professed to be attended to. The investigators were similarly disappointed with their performance in religious instruction and with the fact that in 229 schools the Church Catechism was repeated only once a week.

The Birmingham Statistical Society also regretted inefficient moral and religious instruction in the common day schools for older children, typically from five to twelve years. 'Taken as a whole, the utmost amount of benefit which accrues to the public from this class of schools will include facility in reading and writing, and some knowledge of arithmetic ... '[13]

Those who always seek relative judgements as distinct from those who regard all discrepancies between the real and the ideal (utopian) as inefficiencies will keep a firm comparative grasp of such Dickensian descriptions as the following:

> We noted the grim approaches ... rubbish dumps on waste land nearby; the absence of green playing spaces on or near the school sites; tiny play grounds; gaunt looking children; often poor decorative conditions inside; narrow passages; dark rooms ... books kept unseen in cupboards for lack of space to lay them out ... and sometimes all around, the ingrained grime of generations.

It is not from a desire to be excessively slick but from an almost urgent respect for the need for due perspective that we now

---

13   Ibid., p. 35.

explain that this last quotation comes not from the 1830s but from paragraph 133 of the English Plowden Report: *Children and Their Primary Schools* (1967). One must say immediately that this passage refers only to the worst areas of English schooling today and that improvement plans are already afoot. It serves to show nevertheless the need for comparative institutional judgement, i.e. a comparison of past imperfections with present ones and not with some unattainable ideal. It illustrates also the way in which selective qualitative quotations unbacked by statistical perspective can at all times seriously mislead, and how especially necessary it is to exercise appropriate care when interpreting the evidence of the past.

Several of the local and national reports on nineteenth-century schooling were particularly critical of the frequent lack of credentials among teachers. The only qualification for the employment of so many teachers, complained the Manchester Report, was their unfitness for any other. Such remarks were often inconsistent; for the same investigators later complained that many teachers combined the job of teaching with other occupations (for which they were clearly fitted). They now objected that such teachers were inefficient because they were dissipating their energies. Later in the century, in the Newcastle Commission Report of 1861, one observer protested that so many teachers had 'picked up' their knowledge 'promiscuously' or were combining the trade of school-keeping with another:

> Of the private school masters in Devonport, one had been a blacksmith and afterwards an exciseman, another was a journey-man tanner, a third a clerk in a solicitor's office, a fourth (who was very successful in preparing lads for the competitive examination in the dockyards) keeps an evening

school and works as a dockyard labourer, a fifth was a
seaman, and others had been engaged in other callings.[14]

Another observer found among the teachers grocers, linen
drapers, tailors, attorneys, painters, German, Polish and Italian
refugees, bakers, widows or daughters of clergymen, barristers,
surgeons, housekeepers and dressmakers.[15]

We have commented elsewhere[16] that while the average small
boy would today probably display wistful wonder at the prospect
of having such a colourful variety of experienced adults to teach
him, the nineteenth-century investigator and commentator saw
them as a collection of uncolleged, and therefore untrained, individuals with little redeeming qualities of possible benefit in the
schoolroom. Our comparative institutional approach requires a
comparison with the products of the Victorian teacher training
colleges that eventually did begin to emerge. These colleges have
subsequently been described by one writer as 'pedant factories,
whose machinery efficiently removed whatever traces of interest
in human culture the scholars had somehow picked up earlier in
their careers'.[17] Rote learning frequently became the passageway
through to the teaching profession via these new 'seminaries of
learning', as they were often called.

Dickens, with the aid of his inimitable literary talent, made full
display of the complaint about lack of teacher qualifications.

Although any man who had proved his unfitness for any
other occupation in life, was free, without examinations

---

14   Newcastle Commission Report, 1861, p. 93.

15   Ibid., p. 94.

16   *Education and the State*, p. 167.

17   R. D. Altick, *The English Common Reader*, 1959, p. 162.

or qualification, to open a school anywhere; although
preparation for the functions he undertook, was required
in the surgeon who assisted to bring a boy into the world,
or might one day assist, perhaps, to send him out of it,
in the chemist, the attorney, the butcher, the baker, the
candlestick maker; the whole round of crafts and trades,
the schoolmaster excepted; and although schoolmasters as
a race were blockheads and impostors who might naturally
be expected to spring from such a state of things, and to
flourish in it; these Yorkshire schoolmasters were the lowest
and most rotten round in the whole ladder.[18]

The implication of Dickens's complaint that the typical teacher was 'without examinations or qualification', or that his only qualification for the occupation was his unfitness for any other, was that teachers should be properly instructed and examined in teacher training establishments. By the 1850s such agitation was at last resulting in the creation of an increasing number of such institutions. Their products, however, were then ridiculed by Dickens with at least the same vitriolic indignation as he had previously bestowed upon the untrained. In his *Hard Times*, published in 1854, he describes the instructor of teachers, Mr Thomas Gradgrind, and the new teacher, Mr M'Choakumchild:

'Now, what I want is, Facts. Teach these boys and girls
nothing but Facts. Facts alone are wanted in life. Plant
nothing else, and root out everything else … Stick to Facts,
sir!'

Mr M'Choakumchild … began in his best manner. He
and some one hundred and forty other schoolmasters, had

---

18   Second preface to *Nicholas Nickleby*.

been lately trained at the same time, in the same factory,
on the same principles, like so many pianoforte legs ...
and had answered volumes of head-breaking questions.
Orthography, etymology, syntax, and prosody, biography,
astronomy, geography, and general cosmography, the
sciences of compound proportion, algebra, land-surveying
and levelling, vocal music, and drawing from models,
were all at the ends of his ten chilled fingers... Ah, rather
overdone, M'Choakumchild. If he had only learnt a little
less, how infinitely better he might have taught much more!

Dickens, who never went to university, should have considered carefully how he himself had become literate, despite his humble family circumstances, in the era that preceded 'free' and 'compulsory' education. It is a pity he never lived to experience the public (government) school system that he was agitating for. He might then have pronounced, like Mark Twain, who *did* have the experience, 'Yes, I did have a public schooling; but I never let it interfere with my education.'

4 LIBERTY AND EDUCATION: JOHN STUART MILL'S DILEMMA

E. G. West[1]

The term 'liberty' invokes such universal respect that most modern political economists and moralists endeavour to find a conspicuous place for it somewhere in their systems or prescriptions. But in view of the innumerable senses of this term an insistence on some kind of definition prior to any discussion seems to be justified. For our present purposes attention to two particularly conflicting interpretations will be sufficient. These are sometimes called the 'negative' and the 'positive' notions of liberty.[2] According to the 'negative' notion, my own liberty implies the reduction to a minimum of the deliberate interference of other human beings within the area in which I wish to act. Conversely the absence of liberty, or coercion, is regarded as undesirable because it amounts to the prevention by other persons of my doing what I want. On the other hand, the 'positive' sense of the word 'liberty' consists in the attainment of self-mastery, or, in other words, the release from the domination of 'adverse' influences. This 'slavery' from which men 'liberate' themselves is variously described to include slavery to 'nature', to 'unbridled passions', to 'irrational

---

1   This essay originally appeared in *Philosophy*, the Journal of the Royal Institute of Philosophy, April 1965, and is reprinted by kind permission of Cambridge University Press.

2   See Isaiah Berlin, *The Two Concepts of Liberty*, Oxford, 1958, to which this analysis is much indebted.

impulses', or simply slavery to one's 'lower nature'. 'Positive' liberty is then identified with 'self-realisation' or an awakening into a conscious state of rationality. The fact that it is contended that such a state can often be attained only by the interference of other 'rational' persons who 'liberate' their fellow beings from their 'irrationality' brings this interpretation of liberty into open and striking conflict with liberty in the 'negative' sense.

This conflict will be illustrated with reference to the historical struggle for improvement in the provision of education in the eighteenth and nineteenth centuries. It must be observed first, however, that the already ambiguous notions of liberty became further complicated in this field by their unavoidable connection with another chameleonic term: 'educational reform'. In turn both concepts were found to be inextricably involved in policy proposals that raised questions as to the desirability or otherwise of parliamentary legislation. The kind of liberty that was usually in most men's minds in the context of eighteenth-century education was that which we have described as 'negative' liberty. Accordingly, 'educational reform' usually meant agitation to negate previous legislation that had given predominant control to the Church and state, rather than to make fresh legislation to supplement or replace private initiative. On the other hand, in the century that followed it was liberty in the 'positive' sense which began to dominate the educational scene. 'Educational reform' now called for positive legislation as part of the conscious and deliberate architecture of a new society. Such legislation was designed to set up new and 'necessary' institutions which, allegedly, a more individualistic world had so far failed to produce. Utilitarianism was the main inspiration of this outlook, and by its novel apparatus of 'social engineering' via 'scientific legislation' a prominent place was reserved for the 'liberation' of the masses through specially designed state educational institutions. It was characteristic of these revolutionary blueprints for the new school systems that they typically revealed Bentham's penchant for centralised administration and the economics of large-scale buildings. But the main point to notice is that the 'liberty' of the Benthamites in this sphere was quite different from and indeed opposed to the 'liberty' of the educational radicals such as J. Priestley and W. Godwin in the late eighteenth century.

Before analysing John Stuart Mill's attempt to synthesise these different concepts it will be helpful to examine representative opinions in the works of two of his acquaintances. William Godwin, who was a member of the circle of friends of J. S. Mill's father, James Mill, and a frequent visitor to his home, was perhaps the most vehement upholder of the concept of 'negative' liberty in education which was typical of the late eighteenth century. On the other hand, J. A. Roebuck, who was a member of the younger generation of Utilitarians, and a personal friend of J. S. Mill, seems to have made the first striking claim for the 'positive' concept of educational liberty to be found among the parliamentary speeches in the early nineteenth century.

William Godwin and the case for negative liberty in education

According to Godwin the only true education was self-education. He maintained that men would only begin to fulfil themselves when they saw that there were no obstacles which they could not break down by their own efforts. Education was needed not to instruct mankind, as one of his opponents, T. R. Malthus, wanted to do, but to 'unfold his stores'. But since men had to discover their potentialities by themselves it was a grave hindrance to their development to make the government responsible for their education. Furthermore, Godwin believed that governments were corrupt anyway and provided only too easy a channel for thinkers who were arrogant enough to believe that they had the monopoly on the truth and that their doctrines alone were worthy of forced consumption through the agency of the state. Godwin accused the Benthamites of such arrogance, for instance, in their claim that they could reduce crime by educating the people in the recognition of legal rules, an education that was to be given in special Benthamite schools. Such rules, argued Godwin, should not be manufactured by one section of society such as the Utilitarians and then 'heralded' to the world. The laws were meaningless if they were not equally discoverable by the whole of the people. As another example Godwin would have contended that the population theory of Malthus was not such a profound revelation as to require, as Malthus advocated, a state-initiated education to make universal announcement of it: 'There is no proposition, at present apprehended to be true, so valuable as to justify the introduction of an establishment for the purpose of inculcating it on mankind.'[3] Indeed, Godwin would probably have accused all the contemporary classical economists of hypocrisy in their insistence on the minimum amount of government interference with the freedom of individuals on the ground that each individual knew his own interests best. For, like the physiocrats who preceded them, each classical economist seemed to have in reserve his own private plan for manufacturing the characters of the same

---

3   *Enquiry Concerning Political Justice*, 1796, ch. VIII, 'Of National Education', p. 296.

individuals in the first place, through the exceptional provision of a state educational system, in which his own ideas were to mould individuals to his liking from the start.[4] Godwin would have imposed this indictment more severely upon the Malthusians and Utilitarians than upon Adam Smith, who displayed more hesitation in this whole matter because of his much greater distrust of government. Adam Smith, despite his own predilection for some exceptional measures in education, would have gone a long way with the following three general criticisms of governmental power in the sphere of instruction.

First, objected Godwin: 'All public establishments include in them the idea of permanence. They endeavour, it may be, to secure and diffuse whatever of advantage to society is already known, but forget that more remains to be known.' In time this inertia meant that even obsolete knowledge would continue to be purveyed. But then the public establishments do something far worse: 'They actively restrain the flights of the mind, and fix it in the belief of exploded errors.'[5] Only some 'violent concussion' would oblige the authorities to substitute a new system of philosophy for an old one: '… and then they are as pertinaciously attached to this second doctrine as they were to the first'.[6] Public education always supported prejudice: '… it teaches its pupils not the fortitude that shall bring every proposition to the test of examination, but the art of vindicating such levels as may chance to be previously established'.[7]

---

4   'This just transfers the problem of limiting governmental or social interference from one plane to another.' Jack Lively, *The Social and Political Thought of De Tocqueville*, 1962.

5   *Enquiry Concerning Political Justice*, op. cit., p. 293.

6   Ibid., p. 294.

7   Ibid., p. 295.

Godwin's second criticism stemmed from his conviction that man's activity in doing things for himself was of supreme value in giving him the only sure springs of progress. Whatever others did for him was not done so well: 'It is in our wisdom to incite men to act for themselves, not to retain them in a state of perpetual pupillage. ... This whole proposition of a national education is founded upon a supposition which has been repeatedly refuted in this work, but which has recurred upon us in a thousand forms, that unpatronified truth is inadequate to the purpose of enlightening mankind.'[8]

Godwin's third objection was based on what he thought would be education's 'obvious alliance' with the prevailing national government: 'Before we put so powerful a machine under the direction of so unambiguous an agent, it behoves us to consider well what it is that we do. Government will not fail to employ it to strengthen its hands and perpetuate its institutions.'[9] It was not true, he argued, that youth should be instructed to venerate the virtues of the British constitution. If anything, they should be taught to venerate *truth*. Godwin was here posing a problem that had its contemporary example in Napoleonic France, and which has since been demonstrated in a particularly conspicuous way in the powers of indoctrination wielded by Hitler, Mussolini, Stalin and apparently by leaders in certain parts of Africa today. It was a problem that deeply concerned John Stuart Mill, as we shall see. Godwin contended that if schemes of national education were established at the height of a despotic power, whilst it could not perhaps stifle truth for ever, yet it would be: '... the most formidable

8   Ibid., p. 296.

9   Ibid., p. 297.

and profound contrivance for that purpose that imagination can suggest'.[10] Furthermore, it was no use arguing that in countries in which more liberty prevailed this sort of injury would not take place. At any one time, even under the best government, it was reasonable to assume that there were important errors: '... and a national education has the most direct tendency, to perpetuate those errors, and to form all minds upon one model'.[11]

J. A. Roebuck and the case for positive liberty in education

Among John Stuart Mill's personal friends who represented Benthamism in the new House of Commons immediately after the Reform Act of 1832, one of the most active was J. A. Roebuck. In his autobiography, J. S. Mill wrote of him: 'it is his title to permanent remembrance, that in the very first year during which he sat in Parliament, he originated (or re-originated after the unsuccessful attempt of Mr Brougham) the parliamentary movement for National Education'.[12] Roebuck devoted his crucial speech to Parliament in 1833 to the three following subjects: 'I would first solicit the attention of the House to the more prominent benefits to be obtained by a general education of the people. Secondly, I would endeavour to show why the Government should itself supply this education; and lastly, I shall attempt to trace a rude outline of a plan by which every inhabitant of this empire might receive the instruction requisite for the well-being of society.'[13] With regard to

10   Ibid., p. 298.
11   Ibid., p. 298.
12   J. S. Mill, *Autobiography*, New York, 1944, p. 136.
13   *Hansard*, vol. XX, 1833, cols 139–66.

the first of these subjects, Roebuck argued that the most prominent benefit from state education would be that it would teach people how to be happy and therefore would reduce violence, mischief and political unrest. This, of course, was the orthodox Utilitarian doctrine. Unhappiness existed because people were ignorant of the proper understanding of the circumstances on which their happiness depended: 'let them once understand thoroughly their social condition, and we shall have no more unmeaning discontents – no wild and futile schemes of Reform; we shall not have a stack-burning peasantry – a sturdy pauper population – a monopoly-seeking manufacturing class'.[14]

With regard to his second subject, the reasons why the government should itself supply the education, Roebuck first argued from the authority of the 'most enlightened' countries in Europe, i.e. France and Prussia, which had already accepted the principle. But his main argument was simply based on precedent. Because it was generally accepted, he argued, that the government did some things, it should therefore do others. To maintain the peace of society the government administered justice, for the furtherance of mobility it superintended the roads, and indeed to regulate public morality it passed laws, thus involving itself with the business of training the 'public mind'. Roebuck therefore concluded: 'Inasmuch, then, as this training is among the chief means of regulating public morality as it is one of the chief means of furthering generally the well-being, the happiness of society – insomuch, we may say, without fear of refutation, that the business of education ought to be deemed one of its chief concerns.'[15]

---

14   Ibid.
15   Ibid.

It is at this point that the contrast with Godwin is the most striking. For the latter, happiness could only be the product of self-discovery. The Utilitarians, on the other hand, genuinely believed that they alone could instruct people on how to be happy. In the words of Roebuck: 'The people at present are far too ignorant to render themselves happy ...'[16] It is not surprising that the clash between the two freedoms became fully exposed later in Roebuck's speech. Answering the charge that the state was robbing people of their freedom, Roebuck protested: 'I ask, Sir, in the first place, if it rob the people of *rational* freedom? We every day coerce the people by laws, and rob them of freedom. ... Freedom in itself is not a good thing – it is only good when it leads to good – if it leads to evil, it must be, it is every day, restrained by the most stringent and coercing bonds.'[17] (Emphasis added.)

Freedom for Roebuck was thus indissolubly linked with goodness, and the arbiter of goodness should be the government. If the government were a bad one, asserted Roebuck, then this was an argument for replacing it with a good one. Now in Roebuck's mind there could be no doubt that a good or 'reformed' government was one that consisted largely of Utilitarian philosophers like himself. The charge of intellectual despotism was sidestepped by the persuasiveness of the word 'good'. In this way, therefore, Roebuck demonstrated his version of liberty in education. His was a 'positive' notion of liberty, one that had to be translated and authorised by 'a good Government', that *deus ex machina* of the whole Utilitarian programme. The liberty of W. Godwin, in contrast, preferred full reference to the individual's own choice

16   Ibid.
17   Ibid.

because there was usually no better criterion and it was certainly preferable to reliance on 'good government', which was to him no more than a disembodied abstraction.

So much for the representatives of the two opposing notions of liberty in the first half of the nineteenth century in England. It remains now to examine John Stuart Mill's attempt at reconciliation.

J. S. Mill's special treatment of education

After much serious thought J. S. Mill argued for very special treatment for education and accordingly made the following proposals: first, education was to be made compulsory by law; second, the state was to see that this law was respected not by providing state schools (except in exceptional circumstances) but by instituting a system of examinations. Should a child fail to attain a certain minimum standard then his parents were to be taxed and the proceeds devoted to his continued education. Cases of exceptional poverty were to be met by special financial dispensations from the state earmarked for the payment of subsidies or fees. In the light of our discussion on liberty, it will be interesting to trace the course of Mill's reasoning which led to these conclusions. It will be argued that his deliberations point to an uneasy compromise between the two notions of liberty as represented in Godwin and Roebuck, a compromise which, on the whole, leaned in favour of the Utilitarian doctrine of the latter.

John Stuart Mill is probably the most celebrated champion of what is known as the liberal point of view. This view carries with it in the popular mind the fullest expression of 'negative' liberty as we have defined it above. Deeply embedded in this concept, as we have seen, is the belief that coercion is bad as such, even though it may have to be chosen sometimes as the lesser of evils. The conviction is that there are certain parts of an individual's life where he is entitled to freedom from interference since it is no business of government at all.[18]

This is the view that is commonly associated with Mill's essay *On Liberty* (1859). The following is a key quotation:

> The object of this Essay is to assert one very simple principle, as entitled to govern absolutely the dealings of society with the individual in the way of compulsion and control, whether the means used be physical force in the form of legal penalties, or the moral coercion of public opinion. That principle is, that the sole end for which mankind are warranted, individually or collectively, in interfering with the liberty of action of any of their number, is, self-protection. That the only purpose for which power can be rightfully exercised over any member of a civilised community, against his will, is to prevent harm to others. His own good, either physical or moral, is not a sufficient warrant. He cannot rightfully be compelled to do or forbear because it will be better for him to do so, because it will make him happier, because, in the opinions of others, to do so would be wise, or even right.[19]

Once stated, however, this belief in freedom as a value in itself is not repeated by Mill as much as one would expect. One explanation of this is that he had a second, but quite independent, notion

---

18 Mill's championship of this view has been recently demonstrated by Berlin, op. cit. See also H. L. A. Hart, 'Immorality and Treason', *Listener*, Vol. 62, No. 1583, pp. 162–3. This is a contribution to the debate which was provoked by the report of the Wolfenden Committee on Homosexual Offences and Prostitution.

19 *On Liberty*, Fontana, 1962 edn, p. 135. This edition will be implied henceforth.

of liberty, and one which increasingly occupied him. Liberty was desirable, he thought, because it had a special utility. This took the shape of certain presumed consequences of which Mill approved, such as variety of effort and experiment and the pursuit of self-perfection. Such 'desirable' development, thought Mill, could only arise from dispersed free choice and healthy spontaneity. Again, Mill buttressed his case for liberty with another subordinate argument, the contention that 'each is the best judge and guardian of his own interests'. This proposition, which was widely supported by his fellow classical economists, is again an argument that is independent of the idea of liberty for its own sake, for it is conceivable that if people were not good judges, then liberty could be dispensed with.

However, when we examine Mill's basic case for intervention, that is 'to prevent harm to others', we discover that he moved away considerably from the purely negative concept of liberty. For to be strictly consistent with this notion, the only kind of 'harm to others' that would be relevant is the harm of impeding another's freedom. The only acceptable formula, in other words, would be 'coercion to prevent coercion'.[20] In fact Mill's idea of 'harm to others' is so wide that he fails to conceal his profound and complementary theory of the state with regard to which liberty has only a subordinate role to play. Thus by 'harming' others, Mill sometimes implied physical injury but at others, as with his opinion on offences against decency, he included injury to good manners. Again, harmful treatment to animals was yet another extension of the idea. Apart from this, 'harm' consisted of failing to perform

---

20 The analysis at this point owes much to H. J. McCloskey, 'Mill's Liberalism', *Philosophical Quarterly*, April 1963.

what Mill considered to be 'assignable duties'. One of the most important of these was the 'correct' treatment of dependants, and accordingly the proper education of children was the appropriate duty 'assigned' to the parent.

Mill took it to be the main duty of the state, to protect all individuals regardless of age. He agreed with Roebuck that the power of the parent over his child was delegated by the state. The state could intervene the moment it was established that the parent was abusing this power, i.e. on the grounds of doing harm to others. Such propositions, however, become less clear when subjected to the 'ordeal of definition'. Even charges of extreme physical cruelty are not always easy to establish. But Mill extended the ideas of harm and cruelty to include the act of *neglecting to develop the child's mental faculties.* This implied the belief that each child had a right to a minimum of education: 'Education also, the best which circumstances admit of their receiving, is not a thing which parents or relatives, from indifference, jealousy or avarice, should have it in their power to withhold.'[21] Now even if 'the best education which circumstances allowed' is capable of easy definition, many strict upholders of negative liberty would still question whether it is relevant to a legitimate case of doing harm to others. They may well concede that the state's duty of protection is clearly called on when any of its members is physically obstructed or injured so that his faculties are in some way impaired. But if a parent neglects the education of a child it is not clear that its faculties have been impaired or injured. They may well remain potentially intact and free to be developed by the child at a later stage.

---

21   *Principles of Political Economy*, Ashley edn, 1915, p. 958. All subsequent references will be to this edition.

In any case, a 'minimum education' appropriate to circumstances cannot be rigorously defined in any way that would satisfy all opinion. Education, for instance, is a wider term than formal schooling. J. S. Mill himself expressed the point thus:

> Even if the government could comprehend within itself, in each department, all the most eminent intellectual capacity and active talent of the nation, it would not be the less desirable that the conduct of a large portion of the affairs of the society should be left in the hands of the persons immediately interested in them. The business of life is an essential part of the practical education of a people; without which, book and school instruction, though most necessary and salutary, does not suffice to qualify them for conduct, and for the adaptation of means to ends. Instruction is only one of the desiderata of mental improvement; another almost as indispensable, is a vigorous exercise of the active energies; labour, contrivance, judgment, self-control: and the natural stimulus to these is the difficulties of life.[22]

It seems to follow from this that the person most in contact with the 'difficulties of life' in a child's family environment would be the parent and that he would at least be an appropriate person to consult. To take one example, if in mid-nineteenth-century England (when that country was relatively underdeveloped) a parent had decided that his child leaving school at the age of twelve would have contributed best to his own and to his family's interest, whereas a state official had contended that thirteen years was a more suitable leaving age, it seems that there would have been a case here of honest difference in opinion. Now the plea for the proper ventilation of honest opinion was another important

---

22   Ibid., p. 948.

feature in *On Liberty*. Mill maintained that we should indulge 'false' opinions because of the possibility that they were right. In the case of education, however, Mill himself, in several parts of his writings, reveals a predilection for overruling parental opinion by state decree in order that his own view, or that of a group of educated, 'rational' or cultivated superiors, should predominate. It certainly seems that strong elements of the positive concept of liberty appeared in Mill's work in the context of state protection of infants. For here he does give the impression of having found a wedge to drive between the parent and child so that ultimately the latter could be 'liberated' from the uncultivated influences of the former.

We are given this impression most forcefully when we discover that on the subject of education he throws away completely his subordinate argument for liberty, the argument that 'each is best judge of his own interests'. Ultimately it seems that his main anxiety was not so much that infants could not judge for themselves. His more serious assertion was that most adults could not judge properly either and that therefore freedom must after all be taken away from them at least in this sphere. For this is the first of Mill's major exceptions to the laissez-faire principle which he discussed in *Principles of Political Economy*:

> The uncultivated cannot be competent judges of cultivation.
> Those who most need to be made wiser and better,
> usually desire it least, and, if they desired it, would be
> incapable of finding the way to it by their own lights. It
> will continually happen, on the voluntary system, that, the
> ends not being desired, the means will not be provided
> at all, or that, the persons requiring improvement having
> an imperfect or altogether erroneous conception of what
> they want, the supply called forth by the demand of the

market will be anything but what is really required. Now any well-intentioned and tolerably civilised government may think, without presumption, that it does or ought to possess a degree of cultivation above the average of the community which it rules, and that it should therefore be capable of offering better education and better instruction to the people, than the greater number of them would spontaneously demand. Education, therefore, is one of those things which it is admissible in principle that a government should provide for the people.[23]

These seem to be the words of a philosopher wishing to 'liberate' his fellows into his state of rationality. One certainly does not associate such views with negative liberty. It is a position in which many 'wise men' find themselves. They are persuaded that this is not really a case of coercion, or if it is, it is excusable because in the words of Fichte 'you will later recognise the reasons for what I am doing now'.

In spite of all this, however, J. S. Mill, the popular champion of liberty, shows, in this field, anguished mental struggle over the whole question of state education. The scepticism of a writer like Godwin emerges now and then with so much compulsion as to amount to apparent contradiction with the statements so far examined. Now the ordinary upholder of negative liberty protests

23 Ibid., p. 953. Notice that Mill's complaint concerns the quality, not the quantity, of education. From the evidence of the 1851 Commission on Popular Education, England, which was about the only remaining European country without a national system of education, was still abreast of its neighbours in quantity. The average working-class parent was paying fees for his children's education and this covered one third of the cost. The question was whether the state should subsidise this vast voluntary system, in which the parent's voice was respected, or supersede it with state schools.

against coercion and the word despotism, which is used to convey his dislike of it, is one of the strongest terms in the language. Similarly, in his moments of doubt, Mill feared that even the educational powers of government could lead to despotism and that they needed the same cautious vigilance, if not more, as other powers. Consider this striking 'Godwinian' passage in the essay *On Liberty*:

> A general State education is a mere contrivance for moulding people to be exactly like one another: and as the mould in which it casts them is that which pleases the predominant power in the government, whether this be a monarch, a priesthood, an aristocracy, or the majority of the existing generation; in proportion as it is efficient and successful, it establishes a despotism over the mind, leading by natural tendency to one over the body.[24]

Such statements seem to make meaningless the assertion of the previous quotation that a 'well-intentioned' government should be capable 'of offering better education and better instruction to the people' than they would themselves demand. For if governments in reality turn out to be a current predominant power such as a majority or a priesthood then the 'well-intentioned' government either does not exist or becomes despotically suspect if it does.

To construct practical proposals out of such a dilemma was no easy task for Mill. His final prescriptions show much greater reflection and caution than those of his friend, Roebuck, with whose reasoning nevertheless Mill seems to have gone a considerable way. In his parliamentary speech Roebuck had openly faced the problem with these words: 'It is dangerous, they say, to put

---

24　*On Liberty*, p. 239.

such an instrument as education into the hands of Government; lest thereby the public mind be debauched, and slavish ideas and habits alone be propagated.'[25] Like Mill, Roebuck took the point seriously. But he thought his particular plan avoided this danger:

> ... because, though I propose to make the education of the people a matter of national and not merely individual concern, I should propose that the persons to determine, in the last resort, on the subject matter of instruction, and on whom the actual task of instruction shall fall, should be the people themselves; the people acting, however, in a public, and not in a private capacity.[26]

This solution on the face of it seemed like a conjuring trick. The danger of despotism is magically spirited away if the people after all are to exercise the power. But this scheme, in effect, was the device of shifting the activity of education from the market and the voluntary system to political organisation. Only such a newly enfranchised audience of his day could, however, have accepted the abstract assertion that a political system, even a democratic one, could be interpreted as the rule of the people. A study of Roebuck's subsequent 'machinery' for education shows clearly that his attempt to answer the charge of possible despotism was only superficial. For the supervision of the national schools in the kingdom was to be the duty of a minister of public instruction with cabinet rank. 'He would apportion the sum of money to be given to each district, for masters, for books, and repairs and a hundred other things. Besides this, the Normal Schools [i.e. the teacher training schools] would be wholly under his control, and he would

---

25   *Hansard*, vol. XX, 1833, cols 139–66.
26   Ibid.

select for himself, and on his own responsibility, the masters and governors of each … also, it would be a very important part of his duty to watch over the composition of books of instruction.'[27] Indeed, the general public, even though it paid the requisite taxes, was subsequently told that its guidance was not really important: 'The great object, however, in any plan of general education would be to make *"the most instructed classes"* the guides. … Do what you will, say what we will, this class must guide and govern.'[28] (Emphasis added.)

It is clear, therefore, that in wanting to give the power to 'the people' Roebuck really meant only one section of them, and a section that constituted the 'proper' governing class.

J. S. Mill was much more apprehensive: 'Though a government, therefore, may, and in many cases ought to, establish schools and colleges, it must neither compel nor bribe any person to come to them.'[29] He advocated that a state school should exist, 'if it exist at all, as one among many competing experiments, carried on for the purpose of example and stimulus, to keep the others up to a certain standard of excellence'.[30] But even here it is interesting that Mill still could not conceal the presumption that the state schools would always be the superior pace-makers. He recognised, however, what Roebuck was not so willing to acknowledge – that if the country contained a sufficient number of qualified persons to provide 'government' instruction, as Roebuck's proposed national system implied, then the same resources would be available under the market or voluntary principle 'under the assurance of remu-

---

27 Ibid.
28 Ibid.
29 *Principles of Political Economy*, p. 956.
30 *On Liberty*, p. 240.

neration afforded by the law rendering education compulsory, combined with State aid to those unable to defray the expense'.

Mill agreed with Roebuck that education should be made compulsory. Beyond that, however, he was not so enthusiastic about the type of direct Benthamite apparatus of centralised control that Roebuck had outlined. Mill preferred to support the compulsion of education with the system of enforcement of public examinations to which children from an early age were to be submitted:

> Once in every year the examination should be renewed, with a gradually extending range of subjects, so as to make the universal acquisition and what is more, retention, of a certain minimum of general knowledge virtually compulsory. Beyond that minimum there should be voluntary examinations on all subjects, at which all who came up [to] a certain standard of proficiency might claim a certificate.

Bentham's system of examinations as the price to be paid for the right to vote had been included by Brougham in his educational proposals to Parliament in 1837. J. S. Mill also advocated this idea.

Strictly speaking, this solution did not remove the power of the state over education, it only narrowed it down to the power of those officials who were to be appointed on behalf of the state to set the examinations. Mill thought that this would not matter so long as the examinations were confined to the 'instrumental parts of knowledge' and to the examination of objective facts only. Where higher classes of examinations were concerned: 'The examinations on religion, politics, or other disputed topics, should not turn on the truth or falsehood of opinions, but on the matter of fact that such and such an opinion is held, on such grounds, by such authors, or schools, or churches.'

But the fact that Mill did not enter into further details as to what was to constitute 'a certain minimum of general knowledge', leaving his proposal in the form of a few generalisations, enabled him to escape many of the serious difficulties that lay beneath the surface of his plan. For instance, who was to determine the subjects to be taught? How would one choose between, say, elementary political economy and geography? Could powers of censorship be easily exercised? Suppose that certain individuals had aversions to certain subjects, who would be the arbiter? J. S. Mill himself, for instance, had a particularly strong objection to the teaching of theology and was insistent that national education should be purely secular.[31] Once again we have here the authoritarian overtones of the intellectual paternalist. Certainly such treatment of other people's opinions seemed to contradict the spirit of *On Liberty* as it is popularly conceived.

Altogether, therefore, in the hands of J. S. Mill, the relationship between education and liberty was a complicated and unsettled one, largely because of his difficulty in determining how far education was a means towards liberty and how far it was one of the ends for which liberty existed. While he shared a substantial part of Godwin's reasoning and the latter's dislike of 'patronified truth', yet there was an inner conflict arising partly no doubt from Mill's Platonic and almost religious reverence for knowledge and learning which his father had struggled so hard, in his supreme

---

31　Mill would make no compromise on this point. If the education were to include religion then he would have opposed any bill for national education. Letter to C. Dilke, 1870. See also his letter to T. H. Huxley, 1865, in *The Letters of John Stuart Mill*, H. S. R. Elliott (ed.), 1910.

pedagogic experiment, to build into the person of J. S. Mill himself.[32]

The emergence from this conflict of such pronouncements by J. S. Mill as 'Those who must need to be made wiser and better usually desire it least …'[33] obscures his eloquent plea for the freedom of the individual in the essay *On Liberty*. Such inconsistency is not to be found in Godwin, nor in Kant, who observed: 'Nobody may compel me to be happy in his own way.' Kant really did treat the individual as an end in himself, as the ultimate author of values who needed no prior conditioning by 'superior' people. J. S. Mill's individual in the end therefore is not perfectly free but to some extent manipulated by the Victorian intellectual paternalism of J. S. Mill himself and his own educated middle class. In the end, the negative liberty that Mill strived to establish becomes difficult to distinguish from an intellectual's special brand of positive liberty, i.e. the idea that what truly liberates is knowledge, rationality or culture.

---

32 J. S. Mill was educated entirely by his father, who thus shared Godwin's ardour for private initiative instruction. See I. Cummins, *A Manufactured Man*, 1960.

33 *Principles of Political Economy*, p. 953.

5 THE ECONOMICS OF COMPULSION
E. G. West[1]

The full complexity of the economic consequences of conventional types of compulsion cannot be grasped without some knowledge of historical circumstances. In the era of nineteenth-century social reform there was genuine and growing concern for children who were deprived in all senses – not just in the area of education. All kinds of public policies were devised to discriminate in favour of these children, including measures to protect them from malnutrition, parental cruelty, poor housing, and inadequate clothing. Laws were so operated as to discipline irresponsible parents selectively. Since it was rarely suggested that the delinquent families were in the majority, these *discriminatory* measures were usually considered sufficient. Those parents who were coerced by the law to treat their children better – as in food and raiment – were in effect subject to compulsion, but it was *selective* compulsion.

The case of education developed differently; here *universal* compulsion was applied. At first sight there seems no difference. Universally applicable laws, it will be argued, should not affect responsible families, since they will already be doing what the law wants them to do. Deeper investigation shows there was

---

1   Reprinted by permission of Open Court Publishing Company, a division of Carus Publishing Company, Peru, IL, from *The Twelve Year Sentence* by William F. Rickenbacker (ed.), copyright © 1974 by the Center for Independent Education of the Institute for Humane Studies.

an important difference. In Britain in the 1860s, just before universal compulsion, there was a near-universal system of private fee-paying schools, and the majority of parents were using it. In 1870 it was thought necessary to complement this system with a few government schools ('board schools') in those areas where there was proved insufficiency. In 1880, universal compulsion was legislated. It was next argued that since the government could not force parents to do something they could not afford, schooling should be made 'free'. Free schooling should be available even to the majority of parents who were previously paying for it, as well as to the minority that the legislation was ostensibly aimed at. Free schooling required full subsidisation. It was next argued that only the new government ('board') schools could fully qualify for such treatment. Private schools that were run for a profit should not be aided because this practice would subsidise profit-makers. (This anti-profit principle was incorporated into every piece of nineteenth-century legislation.) Most of the remaining private schools were connected with the Churches. It was argued that it would be wrong to treat these as favourably as the 'board schools' because that would be using Catholic taxpayers' contributions to subsidise Protestant schools and vice versa. The result was that the new 'board schools' originally set up to complement a private system eventually *superseded* it. Many, if not most, of those who originally advocated compulsion were supporters of voluntary Church schools. In the particular way in which compulsion was enacted (universal as distinct from selective compulsion) there were significant effects upon the majority of parents who did not need it. For them it became in effect compulsion to change from one school system to *another*. Since this new (collectivised) system was associated with a growing educationist bureaucracy and a protection-seeking teaching profession that was among the strongest of nineteenth-century agitators for universal compulsion, it is possible that universal compulsion eventually led to less total schooling in real terms, or in terms related to family preference, than would otherwise have resulted (bear in mind that education is a normal good, the supply of which would have increased 'voluntarily' following the increases in income and population that actually occurred after 1880).

The argument that where schooling was made compulsory the government had an obligation to see to it that poor parents could pay the necessary fees goes back as far as the Report on the Handloom Weavers in 1841, which was largely written by Nassau Senior. It appears on page 123: 'It is equally obvious that if the State be bound to require the parent to educate his child, it is bound to see that he has the means to do so.'[2] In his *Principles*, published seven years later, John Stuart Mill similarly argued: 'It is therefore an allowable exercise of the powers of government to impose on parents the legal obligation of giving elementary instruction to children. This, however, cannot fairly be done, without taking measures to insure that such instruction shall always be accessible to them either gratuitously or at a trifling expense.'[3]

Mill's basic case for the establishment of compulsion rested on his belief that the voluntary principle had failed to supply sufficient instruction. '... I shall merely express my conviction that even in quantity it is [in 1848] and is likely to remain altogether insufficient ...'[4]

---

2 *Parliamentary Papers*, vol. X, 1841.
3 *Principles*, Ashley edn, 1915, p. 954.
4 Ibid., p. 955.

Notice that this was not an appeal to systematic evidence. National data was not available until the 1851 Census Report on Education in England and Wales. This revealed in fact over two million day scholars. Mill was arguing from impressionism, from a 'conviction'. He had a very firm opinion that 'the uncultivated can not be competent judges of cultivation'. The voluntary principle failed because '... the end not being desired, the means will not be provided at all ...'[5]

If Mill and his supporters had been more willing to have their views efficiently tested by the evidence, they might not have been so hasty in recommending universal compulsion. Careful reflection would have shown that it was difficult to distinguish between parental 'negligence' and parental indigence. Countless observers in the nineteenth century condemned parents for their irresponsibility, and then, after compulsion was established, urged that the fees should be abolished to enable them to overcome their poverty. The only sure way to disentangle these issues is to subsidise the fees first; only then, after a suitable time lag, will the real preferences of parents reveal themselves. Furthermore, one should add to the total amount available for subsidy the funds that would otherwise be spent on policing a compulsory system.

Empirical studies

Hitherto historians of education have been unanimous that the evidence shows that compulsion did significantly increase attendance in the twenty or thirty years after the legislation. Their argument is inadequate for four reasons. The first relates to the point

5   Ibid., p. 953.

just made. Among the other things that happened in addition to compulsion was the steady reduction of fees. This reduction works in the direction of expanding the demand for schooling (provided that the subsidies do not come entirely from extra taxes on the beneficiaries). Second, the per capita national income was increasing during those years. This means that, provided education was a normal good (with a positive income elasticity of demand),[6] the voluntary demand for it even as a consumption good would have increased anyway. It is true that the opportunity costs of schooling (forgone earnings) would have increased, and this would have worked in the opposite direction. Still other forces were pushing in favour of expansion, however. There was, for instance, a secular decline in loan interest, a circumstance that tends to increase the incentive to invest in more schooling. Again the secular fall in the death rate must have had a similar influence.

Third, there was a steady expansion of population. Growth of voluntary attendance in absolute terms would have occurred for this reason alone. (Several historians do acknowledge this point.) Fourth, many observers have quoted figures of increased enrolment following compulsion at public ('board') schools. Much of this increase, however, was the result of a switching from private schools. The switching occurred because the public schools were increasingly forcing others out of the market by subsidised fees.

In their regression analysis of nineteenth-century compulsory legislation in the USA, Landes and Solmon[7] found that in 1880 the

---

6   i.e. sales volume rises with disposable income: for example, entertainment and travel. An example of *zero* income elasticity of demand might be common salt – *Ed*.

7   W. M. Landes and L. C. Solmon, 'Compulsory Schooling Legislation: An Economic Analysis of the Law and Social Change in the Nineteenth Century', *Journal of Economic History*, March 1972.

average level of schooling was greater in states with compulsory laws than in states without them when other independent variables, such as state income, the number of foreign immigrants, population density, etc., were held constant. But they emphasised that it was not possible to conclude from this that compulsory legislation was the cause of higher levels of schooling. The possibility remained that differences in schooling between states with and without compulsory laws pre-dated these laws. Further investigation revealed that this in fact was the case. They concluded that school legislation was definitely not the cause of higher schooling levels: 'Instead these laws appear to have merely formalized what was already an observed fact; namely, that the vast majority of school age persons had already been obtaining a level of schooling equal to or greater than what was to be later specified by statute.'[8]

In Britain the nineteenth-century data is less accessible and more fragmented. Compulsion was initiated by thousands of local school boards when they were set up after 1870. One has the strong immediate impression that in the short run there was some significant influence. But there were different circumstances in Britain and the USA. In many parts of America universal free schooling was established before compulsion. For instance, in New York State the Free Schools Act finally abolished fees (parental rate bills) in 1867. The New York Education Act establishing compulsion was passed seven years later. In Britain compulsion came first and the trend towards heavily subsidised fees and eventually zero prices came after. The causal connection between compulsion and enrolment is therefore more difficult to elicit in the British case, because the move towards free schooling could have been a strong

---

8   Ibid., section IV.

influence in expanding enrolments. A stronger apparent effect of the compulsory legislation in Britain might therefore be explained in these terms.

Enforcement costs

Our analysis so far has assumed that compulsion is fully enforced. In practice enforcement is a variable; its success is proportional to the resources devoted to it. After the nineteenth-century legislation, truancy did not cease completely; and it has not done so to this day. Indeed, in New York it was reported in 1970 that the Board of Education 'can no longer enforce' the state's compulsory schooling law 'because of the high rate of truancy'.[9] Minimum school laws impose an expected penalty depending on the probability of being caught and the probability of legal proceedings. This cost will vary in subjective terms depending on personal disutility from non-compliance and on risk aversion. If 'too much' compulsion is enforced there is the danger of large-scale parental 'rebellion', and the law is brought into disrepute.

In a paper read before the British Association in the 1870s a Professor Jack questioned the wisdom of the authorities in Birmingham being so proud of their above-average attendance increases. These were obtained, he said, with especially stringent enforcement measures. Whereas the average attendance increase in Glasgow, after compulsion was adopted in that city, was 25 per cent per annum, with prosecutions of one in 20,000 of the popula-

---

9   *New York Times*, 12 February 1970, p. 1. Quoted by Barry Chiswick, 'Minimum Schooling Legislation, Externalities and a "Child Tax"', *Journal of Law and Economics*, 1972.

tion, the average increase in Birmingham was 31 per cent and the prosecutions one in 200.

Joseph Chamberlain retorted that Birmingham was not being tougher than Glasgow. In Scotland, although there were fewer convictions, the penalties were more severe. The actual amount of the Glasgow penalty was in many cases 40 shillings, whereas the maximum penalty in England was five shillings. The fear of the heavier Scottish penalty was an even bigger deterrent.

More interesting in Chamberlain's reply is his argument that the biggest cause of increased attendance in Birmingham was the drastic reduction in school fees. The Birmingham school board was exceptional in these reductions. It had lowered fees in many cases to one penny, whereas the typical board school fee was three pennies. Chamberlain discovered (in economist's jargon) an elasticity of demand for education that was greater than unity:

> As regards the boys' and girls' schools in which the penny fee has been adopted, the result has been very remarkable, and to some of us, at all events, very satisfactory. Wherever the fees have been reduced, the total amount of fees received in a given period after the reduction has exceeded the total amount of fees received … in other words, the reduction of fees in every case has trebled the attendance. … I can only say that my experience since I have sat upon this board confirms me in the opinion that if we could have universal free schools in England, as they exist in America, France, Sweden, Norway, Denmark and many other countries, we should reduce the necessity of compulsion to a minimum, even if we did not do away with it altogether.[10]

---

10   Joseph Chamberlain, 'Six Years of Educational Work in Birmingham', an address delivered to the Birmingham School Board, 2 November 1876, pp. 19–20.

Compulsion and the economics of politics

The findings of Landes and Solmon that school legislation in the USA did not cause higher schooling levels in the nineteenth century leave us with an obvious problem. Why was such an elaborate administration for universal compulsion set up if its achievements were so small? The modern branch of positive economics known as 'the economics of politics' may give some insight. It will be helpful to consider first another example of 'individual failure': inadequate feeding or individual malnutrition.[11] Suppose that two people out of a community of one thousand cannot be trusted to feed themselves or their children adequately and that such irresponsibility is regarded as a social detriment. What is the most viable policy for a politician whose behaviour is attuned to vote maximisation? If a universal degree of compulsion is to be established, this could involve substantial policing costs, including the costs of inspecting and checking not only the eating habits of the two delinquents but also those of the remaining 998. Compare this situation with one wherein, say, about 450 out of the 1,000 are likely to be delinquents. At first sight it may appear that the case for universal (as distinct from selective) compulsion is less substantial in the first situation with two 'delinquents' than in the second with 450. When political considerations enter, however, the position appears more complex. Making nearly half of the electorate do something they have no wish to do is clearly a policy that stands to lose more votes than one that coerces only two people.

The result seems paradoxical. Other things being equal, com-

---

11 The following illustration and parts of the subsequent argument are taken from my *Economics, Education and the Politician*, Hobart Paper 42, Institute of Economic Affairs, London, 1968. This work develops the argument especially in the context of the forthcoming raising of annual leaving age in Britain.

pulsion is more 'profitable' to the government the smaller the minority to be compelled. Yet the needs of the children of a small minority of 'irresponsible' parents may be met more efficiently if the paternalistic powers of government are concentrated on them, and not diffused over wide areas where they are not needed. Ideally, compulsion should be selective and not universal. Where universal compulsion is too readily applied, the authorities may shelter themselves too comfortably from pressures to improve facilities. Where there is no compulsion to stay on at school in the sixteenth or seventeenth year, the suppliers of formal 'education' (the schools) are in competition with informal but efficient alternative forms of education such as apprenticeships and learning on the job. The obligation constantly to 'lure' young people into additional schooling puts constant pressure upon schools and teachers to be imaginative and efficient. Conversely, the protectionist instinct of schools leads them into alliance with governments to support compulsion. This hypothesis was previously put forward in an article in 1967,[12] where it was concluded that in the US context:

> Especially since public money was distributed to the schools and their staffs in proportion to the numbers in attendance, we should expect that the kind of agitation that would next have been undertaken (after fees had been successfully abolished) by the income maximizing teachers, managers and the officials, especially those of average or less than average ability, would have been a campaign for an education that was compulsory by statute.[13]

---

12 E. G. West, 'The Political Economy of American Public School Legislation', *Journal of Law & Economics*, 1967.

13 Ibid., p. 124.

The historical evidence in America supported the hypothesis: 'Serious agitation for compulsory attendance by bureau officials and teachers built *up* very soon after the success of the free school campaign of 1867.'[14]

Landes and Solmon now conclude that their findings are also consistent with this sort of explanation:

> On the demand side, two forces would be at work to increase the demand for compulsory legislation. First teachers and school officials are likely to favour and promote legislation that compels persons to purchase their product; namely schooling. As enrolment and attendance rates rise and the length of the school year increases, the number of teachers and school officials also increases. Along with a growth in their number, we expect an increase in their power to influence legislators to support a compulsory law. On the supply side … with a growth of schooling levels, the number of parents opposed to the enactment of the law would obviously decline.[15]

There is similar evidence in English history. Almost without exception the nineteenth-century government inspectors wanted compulsion.[16] Matthew Arnold, school inspector for the Metropolitan District of Westminster, seems at first sight to have been an exception. In 1867 he thought compulsion was not appropriate to England. 'In Prussia, which is so often quoted, education is not flourishing because it is compulsory, it is compulsory because it is

---

14 Ibid., p. 124.

15 Landes and Solmon, op. cit.

16 See especially the annual reports to the Education Department of W. J. Kennedy (1872), Mr Waddington (1872), Mr Bowstead (1871), Rev. F. Watkins (1872), Rev. F. F. Cornish (1882), J. G. Fitch (1882), G. H. Gordon (1882).

flourishing.... When instruction is valued in this country as it is in Germany it may be made obligatory here ...'[17] This objection obviously related only to the question of timing; compulsion should be established when everybody, or nearly everybody, prized culture so much that voluntary instruction would be universal. The question as to why the 'means' of universal compulsion should be applied after the 'ends' had already largely been obtained was not raised by Arnold. It was in the interests of his fellow inspectors and his department that it was not. But despite his doubts about direct compulsion, Arnold was a strong advocate of indirect compulsion. This, in 1867, was the better expedient: 'The persevering extension of provisions for the schooling of all children employed in any kind of labour is probably the best and most practicable way of making education obligatory that we can at present take.'[18]

Along with the Inspectorate and the Education Department, the proprietors of schools also advocated compulsion. While the voluntary school managers objected to the setting up of board schools that were able to compete unfairly, they were not opposed to the setting up of school *boards* where this was done (as the act allowed) to organise compulsion and finance to help the poor pay the voluntary school fees. Mr Bowstead in his report testified to this attitude: 'It by no means follows that, if once such a supply of voluntary schools were secured, the same objections would continue to be raised to the establishment of school boards. On the contrary there is among school managers, both lay and clerical, a very strong desire to be armed with the powers conferred upon school boards by the recent statute.'[19]

---

17 Matthew Arnold's Report for 1867.
18 Ibid.
19 Mr Bowstead's General Report for 1871.

If compulsion does cause (or prolong) lethargy among mono-poly suppliers of schooling, the reform will be perverse. This point was grasped a century ago in America. When, in 1871, the school suppliers of education in New York State were lamenting their loss of income because of 'early leaving', the superintendent remonstrated:

> It is palpable that the prominent defect, that calls for
> speedy reformation, is not incomplete attendance, but
> poor teaching … I speak of the needed improvement in
> the particular mentioned, in comparison with compulsion,
> as a means of securing attendance; and I contend that,
> before sending out ministers of the law to force children to
> school, we should place genuine teachers in the school room
> to attract them … the improvement in question should
> be made before resorting to the doubtful experiment of
> compulsion. It cannot be done suddenly by legislation.[20]

The superintendent's proposal, however, was defeated. The influence of the teachers' political lobby was already too strong for him.

It is consistent with the hypothesis of political 'profit (vote) maximising' that politicians under pressure from, or in alliance with, the factor supply interest groups will have an incentive to make the electorate believe that the problem of delinquency is greater than it really is. One way of fostering this illusion is to make each parent think that, in confidence, compulsion is not intended for *his* particular children; for this would indeed be a reflection on the parent in question and the politician does not want to alienate him. The politician will be on better ground if he

---

20 Annual Report of the New York Superintendent of Public Instruction, 1871.

suggests that compulsion is perhaps really needed for some of his (unspecified) neighbours who are less obviously reliable. Indeed, it is possible that in such a way the more compulsion that is established the more the 'good' individual families may believe that 'bad' families exist. By such a process, the status of the politician grows in proportion as that of 'the average parent' deteriorates.

The supposed 'need' to raise the compulsory leaving age in Britain affords an interesting example. For an objective observer the key information is the precise number of *actual* 'delinquents' who would fail to stay on voluntarily. Conventional questionnaires often yield information on this that is too superficial. The measure of the parental demand for education should relate to *efficient* education. A measure that expresses the willingness to stick with inefficient surroundings is a quite different and inadequate one. All British observers, including the politicians, have admitted in the last ten years that schools have been overstretched, buildings substandard, and teachers too few. The true numbers 'who wish to stay on' cannot adequately be assessed until they have been given effective opportunities, and time, to decline the offer of efficient and available facilities. As the Crowther Report put it in 1959: '... good educational facilities, once provided, are not left unused; they discover or create a demand that public opinion in the past has been *slow* to believe existed ... many boys and girls are at present deprived of educational facilities which they would use well and which they are legally entitled to receive'.[21]

Since 1959 the demand for schooling has been increasing in proportion to the supply of facilities. In these circumstances it is

---

21 '15 to 18, A Report of the Central Advisory Council for Education (England)', 1959, para. 100.

certainly not easy to say to what extent 'compulsion' is a necessary additional stimulus to the provision of good facilities. We cannot know with any accuracy until those facilities are provided. Meanwhile, emphasis upon compulsion may be 'politically expedient', but to the citizen it may well be dangerous in that it may involve a wrong definition of the problem.

Normative welfare economics

So far we have employed positive economics; this proceeds by prediction and the testing of hypotheses with the facts. Normative economics, to which we now turn, is concerned with what 'ought to be' rather than with what is. Traditional normative analysis has been rooted in the welfare economics of Pareto, which assumes that each individual is to count and that each is the best judge of his own interest. A Pareto optimum point is one where any change will harm at least one person in society. A Pareto optimum move is one that benefits at least one person and harms nobody.

In one sense, if we take the family to be the basic unit, and if the new laws are to 'bite', the establishment of compulsion will not pass the Pareto criteria because it will injure some individuals; it will not be a Pareto move. It is possible, however, to achieve a given level of schooling without injury if simultaneous compensation is paid. If compulsion is accompanied by the introduction of 'free' education, the financial benefit of the reduced education costs to the family may provide this compensation. The family could rationally vote for such a move (although there is still considerable fiscal illusion concerning which taxpayers pay for what). The direct expenses of schooling (the fees) are not the only costs, however. In some cases, indirect costs, notably in the shape of the loss of forgone earnings, will be critical. While the social benefits are positive, the private benefits may be negative. With reference to low achievers, W. Hansen, B. A. Weisbrod and W. Scanlon have concluded, 'They are unlikely to benefit financially unless an attempt is made to insure that they offer valuable opportunities, such as training programmes, to enhance their earning power.'[22] In all these cases it will be necessary to compensate the family not only with schooling subsidies (or vouchers) but also with income replenishments.[23] It should be emphasised that where compulsion *is* accompanied by appropriate compensation it no longer has the implications of strong coercion. Where income supplements are given to encourage schooling, the function of compulsion is similar to the 'compulsion' implied in any contract to deliver goods or to provide specific services.

If there is a genuine redistribution, that is if the beneficiaries are receiving 'subsidies' that are not financed through taxes upon themselves, normative welfare economics must explore the possible motives of those in society who voluntarily vote to have funds transferred away from them for the schooling of others. One common explanation is that the consumption of schooling by one person in Group A enters measurably into the utility of those persons making up Group B. In other words there are interdependent utility functions. Another explanation is that education provides external benefits to Group B. These externalities, however, are

---

22 W. Hansen, B. A. Weisbrod and W. Scanlon, 'Schooling and Earnings of Low Achievers', *AER* LX(3), June 1970, p. 417. See also the subsequent comments by Barry Chiswick, Stanley Masters and Thomas Ribich, and the reply by Hansen et al., *AER* LX11(4), September 1972, p. 752.

23 For further details, see E. G. West, 'Subsidized but Compulsory Consumption Goods: Some Special Cases', *Kyklos*, 1971.

never specified very precisely, and there is a dearth of supporting evidence. Usually writers confine themselves to a *presumption* that they exist and give one or two possible illustrations. The most popular example is that an 'educated' child will be more law-abiding. This assumption has been examined empirically elsewhere[24] and it has been shown that the evidence does not support it. In any case, the idea has always seemed ambiguous. If a member of a neighbouring family invades or damages my property, I normally look to the law for compensation. It is held in the present instance, however, that I should compensate the potential trespassers with school subsidies in the hope that this will reduce the probability of their damaging me. This seems a curious external benefit.

Compulsion as a constitutional provision

Instead of naked coercion, let us now examine the 'constitutional approach'. Each individual is treated as a choice-maker in his selection from basic sets of legal frameworks. Every individual is now a decision-maker not only in the marketplace and at the ballot box but also in the setting up of the basic constitution that lays down the ground rules within the chosen democratic system. Imagine a new community settlement of young immigrant adults where no children have yet been born and no constitution has yet been laid down. Each adult will now have to consider not only his future private utility of having children but also the potential disutility from the 'undesirable' behaviour or appearance of the neighbour's children. Since the neighbour will be in the reverse position (fearing the potential disutility from one's own children), a constitutional

24   E. G. West, *Education and the State*, 2nd ed., 1970, ch. 3.

rule may be agreed, laying down the conditions in which the 'privileges of parenthood' shall be conferred. One of these conditions will be that each parent will supply a given minimum of education, food, clothing, and so on, from his own resources. If society depends exclusively on these conditions to protect children and to provide sufficient external benefits, then no subsidies, income transfers or price reductions will be necessary for any of the goods and services mentioned. Because of the anticipated legal responsibilities, adults will be discouraged from marriage or parenthood until they can afford to bring their children up in conformity with the minimum constitutional standards. Pareto's 'optimality' will now be achieved by a preliminary and unanimous agreement to abide by the chosen democratic rules. Compulsion will still be a principle in schooling, but it will be compulsion of parents to purchase schooling, like other necessities, in the upbringing of their children. Schooling will be positively priced.

The community could of course also choose to have a 'second line of defence' in the form of occasional subsidies or income transfers to meet the needs of marginal (insurance-type) cases, such as those where families become suddenly destitute. Clearly we have now isolated two polar cases. The first is the circumstance of constitutional compulsion where the adult is previously contracted to full responsibility for prerequisite levels of consumption of externality-generating goods. The second is the opposite, where the community accepts full responsibility and supplies these goods free of charge together with compensatory income transfers where necessary. In the second case, 'compulsion' is of an emasculated kind.

Does this 'constitutional explanation' hold good? Conceptually there is a problem of infinite regress – of knowing which individual preferences to respect: those at the constitutional stage or those where the individual wants to rebel at some subsequent period. Again in the real world we observe piecemeal plans and a combination of devices. While families are expected to clothe their children adequately, children's apparel is not, as is schooling, made free to all; neither are there (with respect to clothing) any universally compulsory laws fully equivalent to those related to schooling. True, there are 'child abuse' laws requiring minimum standards of consumption of food and clothing. As distinct from the way schooling is customarily provided, however, no financial benefits exist to supplement the operation of these laws directly, although welfare or child assistance subsidies probably have that effect. Nor are there specific subsidies for the housing of children. Parents expect that they have to face obligations to purchase food for their offspring at positive prices. School lunches are often subsidised, it is true, but rarely are they so fully subsidised as to allow consumers to enjoy zero prices. School lunches, moreover, are not subsidised on non-school days. It is evident that some rough conformity with the polar cases or normative welfare principles previously outlined does appear here and there. The principles upon which mixtures of these cases appear are, however, quite obscure.

Free education: who benefited?

We come back to the fact that the real world contains far from 'perfect' political processes. This being so, the constitutional dimension of our problem merges once more with the economics of politics or, in this case, 'imperfect' politics. Vote-gaining behaviour in an oligopolistic political structure could well be of significant explanatory value. An extension of compulsion may improve the image of a political party even though few individual families suffer disutility. By anticipating future national income increases, a government may announce plans for raising the compulsory school period years ahead. In doing so, it need antagonise very few, since, to repeat, compulsion may simply underline what most people would do anyway.

We have to return to the 1870s in England to discover the circumstances in which these important issues were openly confronted. Helena Fawcett and her husband, Henry Fawcett, Professor of Political Economy at Cambridge,[25] both represented what we have called the constitutional view. They both strongly urged compulsion but threw down the challenge that if schooling was to be made free, so too should food and clothing. If free schooling was to be adopted, they insisted, it should be openly acknowledged to be another form of relief; and the danger should be faced that, like free food and clothing, free schooling would eventually pauperise the whole community. Sir Charles Dilke, spokesman for the 'non-constitutionalists' in the Birmingham League (the pressure group for compulsory, free and non-sectarian schooling), took strong objection. Helena Fawcett's reasoning, he argued, was the '*reductio ad absurdum* of some of the oldest principles of science to degrade the people in order to maintain an economic theory'.[26] The analogy between free schooling and free food was a false one, Dilke said. Intervention to save a child from starvation was a justifiable protection of an *individual* – protection of an individual member of society who was incapable of protecting himself. Free and compulsory schooling, on the other hand, was justifiable because

---

25 He was Alfred Marshall's predecessor in the Cambridge chair.

26 Sir Charles Dilke, Report of the Third Annual Meeting of the National Educational League held in Birmingham, 17 and 18 October 1871.

it protected the society. 'The state suffers by crime and outrage, the results of ignorance. It interferes, therefore, to protect itself.'[27] This identification of the poor sections of society with the criminal class was widespread among the Victorian gentility. Dilke and his associates in the Birmingham League did not consider for one moment the possibility that they also (like Mrs Fawcett) were 'degrading the people in order to maintain an economic theory'.[28]

In addition to the crime reduction argument, free and compulsory schooling was connected with the need for national defence. As Dilke put it: '… education comes far nearer to drill than it does to clothes. Drill, or compulsory service of all citizens in time of emergency, may become a state necessity'.[29]

The military success of Prussia against France in 1870 was clearly uppermost in their minds. Jesse Collins, the secretary of the Birmingham League, echoed Dilke's sentiments:

> … the policy of the country on critical occasions, involving war or any other calamity, has to be determined by the people, and it is of the greatest national importance that they should be fitted by education to exercise an intelligent judgement on any subject submitted to their decision … all are taxed for the maintenance of the army, navy, and police, because all share in the benefits these institutions are supposed to afford, and would have to share in the loss and inconvenience resulting from their non-existence; and by the same rule all should be taxed for the support of schools because all share in the increased wealth, security, and general advantages resulting from the education of the

---

27 Ibid.
28 Dilke's arguments were repeated, especially by Joseph Chamberlain, Jesse Collins and Edwin Chadwick.
29 Dilke, op. cit., p. 157.

people, and have also to share the expense and danger of crime and other results of ignorance.[30]

The argument so far, however, had not really destroyed the analogy of schooling with food and clothing. A half-starved, half-clad population would be just as useless in defence as a half-educated one. Joseph Chamberlain added another argument that seemed more consistent. Food was a necessity for existence, but schooling was not a necessity at all: 'Human nature, which was almost perpetually hungry, might be trusted to supply itself with the elements of bare existence; but human nature could not be trusted to supply itself with instruction, of which a great many human beings had, unfortunately, a very low opinion.'[31]

One missing element in Chamberlain's theory was attention to the problem of how such an 'irresponsible' population could be relied upon to vote for politicians like himself who wanted to regiment them, now that democracy had largely arrived (with 1867 enfranchisement). It was not just a question of 'educating our masters'; there was the problem of politically persuading the 'masters' to elect their mentors. Chamberlain imputed irresponsibility to 'a great many human beings'. A great many more, indeed the majority of families, had proved that they did have a high opinion of schooling. In 1869 most parents were buying it directly, most families were already sending their children to school without being compelled, most school leavers were literate, and most of 'our masters', in other words, were already being educated of their

---

30   Jesse Collins, *Remarks on the Establishment of Common Schools in England*, 1872.
31   Joseph Chamberlain, 'Free Schools', address to the Birmingham School Board, 18 June 1875.

own free will.[32] The argument for compulsion applied at most to only a small minority of families.

But the Birmingham League supporters meant something more in their arguments. The 'human nature' that 'would not be trusted to supply itself with instruction' was really at fault because it could not supply itself with the *right sort of instruction*. It had allowed itself to be given a schooling that was connected with religious organisations – especially of Anglican persuasion. The Birmingham League was an expression of the newer secular nationalism of the nineteenth century. It included many whom the twentieth century could now describe as 'false optimists'. The system of compulsion they had in mind included compelling people to change from sectarian to secular (or non-sectarian) schools. They knew that this could not be accomplished by direct means; other groups had to be reckoned with – High Tories, for instance, believed that only a school controlled by the established Church could be effective in improving morality and decreasing crime. The methods adopted by the League involved the strategic use of the new 'board schools', which were established by the Education Act of 1870 to fill gaps in the voluntary system of denominational and other private schools. Soon after 1870 these new institutions, which were largely non-sectarian if not secular, were beginning to price many of the Church schools out of the field. This was a consequence of the board schools' ability to draw heavily upon the 'rates' (local property taxes) and so survive and win any competition. Church schools, the League argued, should not be supported

---

32 Most people still find these facts surprising. Yet they are facts; and they have been obscured by years of 'official' and 'quasi-official' histories of education. See E. G. West, *Education and the State*, op. cit. Also *Education and the Industrial Revolution*, Batsford, London, 1975.

by the 'rates', because that would involve the objectionable practice of subsidising religions. People should pay for their religious instruction separately.

In 1875, the Reverend F. S. Dale spoke up against the campaign of the Birmingham League for universally free schools. He did not oppose the *selective* remission of burdens upon the poor but complained that the League's desire for *universally* free schooling (in the new board schools) was a desire to undermine the 1870 Education Act and destroy existing schools. 'Free schools were part of yet a greater scheme, when the Church of England should be thrown over.'[33] Jesse Collins, on behalf of the League, made the following candid reply (here in reported speech):

> With regard to Mr F. S. Dale's assertion that the free system would close the voluntary schools – denominational schools was the best name – he quite admitted, and he thought they ought not to deny, that, in so far as they were sectarian institutions, or remained for sectarian purposes, the free system would kill them. It was the pure Darwinian theory – the fittest only would survive. If education was the object, then the free scheme got them out of all their difficulties, because they could not deny that by the free system under the school board a better education would be given than could possibly be given by the voluntary schools, on account of their precarious income ...[34]

Edwin Chadwick also supported compulsory attendance provided it was at the right (i.e. the 'nationalised') schools. He

---

33 Meeting of the Birmingham School Board, 18 June 1875.

34 Ibid. 'The survival of the fittest' analogy was obscure; in the Darwinian scheme it was not a matter of subsidised animals surviving the non-subsidised, or the heavily subsidised surviving the weakly subsidised.

complained that the small sectarian schools did not provide the appropriate secular curriculum: 'The experience is now accumulating of the great disadvantages of the small separate schools.' In the large schools subsidised or established or controlled by governments there were the 'superior' attractions of 'gymnastic exercises, the drill, elementary drawing, music, military fetes and parades, to which the small sectarian could not obtain ....'[35]

Clearly this survey has brought the special circumstances of politics well into the picture. From simple normative economics it is conceivable that the public might vote to live under a constitution that provides compulsory, free and secular schools that are primarily designed to ensure military protection and domestic order. Each individual will then express his own preferences *ex ante*. It is arguable that, *ex post*, compulsion could thus be reconciled with the tradition of respect for individual preference that the welfare economics of Pareto endorses. The most elementary reference to the historical record encourages doubt as to whether there was anything like a popularly articulated preference for the system that evolved. The positive economics of politics (especially the politics of pressure groups) seems to explain more than the normative economics of voluntary constitutions.

It has been shown that historically compulsion in Britain was closely interrelated with the issue of 'free' schooling. Both compulsion and free provision were introduced in such special ways as to suggest that the general public were more manipulated than consulted. There is in fact no known English record of direct consultation of individual families to discover their wishes in the late

---

35   Edwin Chadwick, 'National Education: A letter thereon to the Lord President of the Council', 1870.

nineteenth century. There *is* such a record concerning their views as to the desirability of 'free' education. This was contained in the intensive nineteenth-century survey of education by the Newcastle Commission. It reported in 1861: 'Almost all the evidence goes to show that though the offer of gratuitous education might be accepted by a certain proportion of the parents, it would in general be otherwise. The sentiment of independence is strong, and it is wounded by the offer of an absolutely gratuitous education.'[36]

Such evidence was not good enough for Jesse Collins, the enthusiast and propagandist for American-type Common Schools, and secretary of the Birmingham League pressure group that eventually had such important influence. It will be fitting to conclude with the sentiments he expressed on the eve of the League's establishment:

> It is frequently urged that the public mind is not yet ripe
> for such laws as free public schools would necessitate, and
> that it is unwise to legislate so much in advance of public
> opinion. The public mind is more easily led in a right
> direction than Government sometimes wish it to be, and
> in this instance, if fairly tested would probably be found
> fully under the idea of a National system of compulsory,
> unsectarian education ... and this reveals the necessity
> for the immediate formation of a Society, National in
> its name and constitution, refusing all compromise, but
> adopting as its platform – *National, secular (or unsectarian)*
> *education, compulsory as to rating and attendance, with state*
> *aid and inspection, and local management.* The action of such
> a Society would be similar to that of the Anti-Corn Law
> League, and its success as certain; by lectures, by writing, by
> agitation in every town, it would give direction and voice to

---

36   1861 Report, vol. 1, p. 73.

> the fresh and ever-increasing interest felt by the people in
> this matter.[37]

Whether 'fresh and ever-increasing interest' was eventually felt by the people has never been demonstrated. Certainly the politicians did find voters to support their programmes of free and compulsory 'education', but that is not necessarily the same thing. Compulsion in 'education' can mean many things and can be applied in several ways and with a variety of consequences. The strongest nineteenth-century motivation behind the politically expressed 'need' for compulsion in Britain was a desire to compel the majority to secularise their 'education'. To do this, compulsion had to be what we shall describe (for want of a better word) as 'universal compulsion'. This denotes an 'ambitious', consciously decided or comprehensive piece of legislation that is embodied in a statute about compulsion per se. We shall distinguish this from the type of compulsion that is usually implicit in ordinary child abuse laws that attempt to deal with cases on a more ad hoc basis. Such provision we have called 'selective' compulsion.

'Selective' compulsion could certainly meet problems caused by a minority of delinquents or poor families; but this would not reduce the power of the Church and the free choice of schools by the majority of parents. Reduced parental choice, in fact, to repeat, was the consequence of 'universal' compulsion because it was coupled with a policy of making the schools 'free'. Free choice was curtailed because only secular schools qualified to be 'free'.

'Selective' compulsion can be a constructive, proper and hu-

---

37 Written in 1867, this passage is contained in Jesse Collins, *Remarks on the Establishment of Common Schools in England*, 1872, pp. 46–7. The italics are in the original.

mane provision in society. To many who support this idea, how-ever, 'universal' compulsion, as described above, will have indirect costs that are so severe as to outweigh the benefits. Modern politi-cal circumstances nevertheless seem unconducive to these senti-ments. It may be, as Jesse Collins believed, that the 'public mind' is more easily led than most people think. And this could be more likely after a hundred years of uniform 'education' in compulsory public schools.

6 EDUCATION AND CRIME: A POLITICAL ECONOMY OF INTERDEPENDENCE
E. G. West[1]

The main assumptions that underlie our public education systems were first articulated and debated during distant historical periods. Sometimes, the records of these debates can stimulate us to reconsider policies that now pervade our society. Furthermore, reconsidering these ancient controversies may even help us to pursue and identify contemporary evidence which can be used to reassess their pros and cons. But such an approach is not simply a matter of second-guessing the dead. More importantly, a judicious mix of historicalism and current evidence can help us to break new intellectual ground.

This paper starts with a consideration of some disputed education issues in early-nineteenth-century England. Though this scene is distant in space, as well as time, the issues involved were especially relevant to our present concerns. The debate was about the forms of educational institutions that would help generate good character in the young. And the ultimate conclusions I reach, from first starting in the past, touch on contemporary American education proposals such as education vouchers and tax deductions to assist parents to buy private education. But, first, we must go back.

---

1   Originally published in the US monthly journal *Character* 1(8), June 1980.

The shaping of English public education

Modern attempts to dissect the nature of 'character' in individuals usually acknowledge some residual mystique beyond the reach of the investigator's tools of analysis. In contrast, in the early 1800s, scholars seemed to be confident that they knew, or would soon know, all there was to know about character. Not only would 'character' be easily analysed, it could also be deliberately created by appropriate institutions, especially the schools.

Consider the views, for instance, of the English intellectual James Mill (the father of John Stuart Mill). His overall character-shaping programme united Bentham's 'pleasure/pain' system of education with the French 'associationist' psychology of Helvetius. Mill made the assumption that the whole of our mental life is based upon responses or reflexes conditional upon physical or mental stimuli. As a result, he thought it was scientifically possible for a system of education to form model citizens with the 'character' of one's choosing. He felt that men certainly would continue to pursue pleasure, but those pursuits could be encouraged which also gave pleasure (or avoided harm) to others. Such was the reasoning in James Mill's celebrated article on education in the *Encyclopaedia Britannica* in 1818.

In retrospect it is easy to expose the innocence and naivety of yesterday's 'social science'. Even if, as Mill proposed, the world was ruled by science, one can still predict that the conflicting opinions of scientists themselves would have eventually disturbed his confident optimism. Certainly the social science of psychology (which Mill helped to found), which has conspicuously affected all types of education, has not been characterised by the unanimity he expected. In any case, society is not ruled exclusively by science, but is led also by philosophy, sentiment, emotion, and religion.

For this reason, the conflicts concerning the generation of 'true' character inevitably become still deeper. And since our society professes to be a democracy, it is obliged to allow minorities the daily opportunity of expressing and influencing others with their own opinion. And these expressions disclose that widely varied opinions exist about so-called moral issues. Under such circumstances, morality certainly cannot be legislated as if it were the outcome of science.

Consider the question, for instance, of the right kind of schooling. Should religion be allowed to play a part in such schooling? This question was intensively debated in England during the nineteenth century. Interestingly enough, debates of a somewhat similar nature also surrounded the development of the Common School movement in America during the same pre-Victorian (or early Victorian) era. But perhaps the English debates displayed greater sophistication, owing to the fact that they occurred on a national level – in part, they transpired in Parliament – not at local and state levels, as in America.

The Utilitarian philosophers James Mill and Jeremy Bentham both favoured widespread government support of (and control over) secular education. But this position excited the opposition of the Dissenters, the Church groups essentially critical of the Church of England and in the forefront of the effort to promote state support of education. Mill and Bentham, to win popular support for their views, entered into a temporary compromise with them and offered a plan providing for non-denominational religious teaching. But the Utilitarians' *ultimate* target was a national system of completely secular education. The religious groups, it was hoped, would be ultimately outmanoeuvred.

We should realise that, while these intellectual manoeuvrings were occurring, England did not have a state-supported school system. The existing mass-based schools were financed by parental payments and private (usually Church-related) contributions. The Utilitarians (who were simultaneously philosophers, publicists and the advisers of politicians) were engaged in a semi-hypothetical exercise, aimed at delineating the elements of a model state-assisted mass education system.

When Parliament passed the Reform Act of 1832, the Utilitarians took this as a sign that there was a climate sympathetic to their educational aims. As a result, their parliamentary spokesman, W. A. Roebuck, proposed that the English government actively intervene in mass education. He attempted to show the House not only the substantial benefits that generally flow from education, but also 'why Government should itself supply this education'. He argued that state education would lead to a reduction of crime: '… as mere matter of police, the education of the people ought to be considered as a part of the duties of the Government'. Yet his 'police' argument was the minimal basis for government schooling. The more elevated basis was the duty of government 'directly to promote good'. And, in those days, as suffrage in England was steadily being expanded, there was anxiety that people should be properly instructed before they were allowed, eventually, to have the vote. In Roebuck's words in Parliament: 'People at present are far too ignorant to render themselves happy even though they should possess supreme power tomorrow.'

But in 1833, the year that Roebuck was presenting his Education Bill in the Commons, education (without government economic support) had widely spread among all the ranks of society. The majority of males, for instance, were already literate. Furthermore, it is interesting that William Cobbett opposed Roebuck during the debates on the ground that crime in England was even then increasing at the same time education was spreading through private support. 'If so, what reason was there to tax the people for the increase of education?'

The Utilitarians were well aware of the spread of privately supported, Church-related education. They believed, however, that it was the *wrong* sort of education, a sort that would certainly not reduce crime. Their objective, therefore, was to wrest ultimate control of education from the religious authorities. Furthermore, in addition to 'undermining' religion in education, they also hoped (at least temporarily) to lessen parental control over children and their education. And, during this period, such parental control was very powerful; over half the costs of education, even among the lower classes, were paid directly by parents – and because of such payments, schools assiduously supported the goals valued by parents.

The historic debate between Cobbett and Roebuck, therefore, resolves itself in the question: Do public (state) schools reduce crime more effectively than do private (mainly religious) schools? While the debate occurred in England, it also has ramifications for our country, and for our period. 'Crime', in a sense, is a synonym for general patterns of poor compared with good character development. And we are faced with contemporary controversies about whether public or private schools are doing better jobs in character development and whether we should expand or diminish our commitment to public sector education.

The debate between Cobbett and Roebuck was pervaded by many generalisations. In contrast to such vagueness, we should now be able to assess the comparative crime-preventing merits of public and private schools more systematically, owing to the accumulation of recorded facts and the increasing sophistication of statistical analysis.

Crime and the schools: some statistical background

The nineteenth-century Utilitarians planned for a school where children were systematically controlled and instructed in an orderly environment so that when they were old enough to leave they would be a help instead of a menace to society. The most striking modern fact in this context is that the crime and violence the Utilitarians wanted to subdue (and exclude) have now entered the very portals of the public school itself.

An analysis of data from 26 cities in the US Law Enforcement Administration's *National Crime Survey* shows that the risk of violence to teenagers is greater in schools than elsewhere. Forty per cent of the robberies and 36 per cent of the assaults on the urban teenagers surveyed (who all attended public schools) occur in schools. The risks are especially high for youths aged twelve to fifteen. Indeed, 68 per cent of the robberies and 50 per cent of the assaults on youngsters of this age occur at school. From the reports of public school *students* collected by the National Institute of Education (NIE) in 1976, it has been found that theft (largely from students by students) is easily the most widespread of in-school offences. Nearly two and a half million of the nation's secondary school students have something worth more than a dollar stolen from them in a month. An estimated 282,000 secondary school students reported that they were attacked at school in a typical one-month period. The proportion was twice as high in junior high schools as in senior high schools. The risk of serious attack is greater in urban areas than elsewhere. For the typical public secondary school student, it was estimated that he or she has about one chance in nine of having something stolen in a month; one chance in 80 of being attacked; and one chance in 200 of being robbed.

The human costs of school-related crime are greater than the reported economic costs. Because of fears for personal safety, teachers fulfil their duties less effectively, and students who spend their days at school afraid are not likely to learn much. The NIE investigations found, among other things, that 800,000 students stayed home from school at least once in the previous month because they were afraid, 12 per cent of the secondary school teachers (or 120,000) said they were threatened with injury by students at school; a similar number said they hesitated to confront misbehaving students because of fear, and almost half of the teachers reported that some students had insulted them or made obscene gestures at them in the last month.

Ironically, for the nineteenth-century Utilitarians, school was a place of instruction to prevent the young from resorting to crime when they *left* school. The criminal, in other words, was thought to be typically a member of the adult class. Current facts present an entirely different picture. According to a 1974 FBI report, 22.2 per cent of total arrests for violent crimes, and 48.1 per cent of total arrests for property crimes (in 1973), were made of individuals aged eleven to seventeen, which is the usual period for enrolment in junior and senior high school. Yet only approximately 14 per cent of the US population is in this age range.

Sociologists and psychologists in the recent past have conducted extensive studies that attempt to describe young offenders and the source of their problems. However, the subject of serious deviant behaviour *in schools* has only recently come to attention.

But although some new work is beginning on how schools may respond to the problem, hardly anything has been done in the way of attempting to answer the question that is rooted in nineteenth-century history. Is there a significant difference in the effects of public schooling compared to private schooling?

Are the effects of American private schools different?

Let us start off by noting that the pattern of income distribution among the families of American contemporary private school students is remarkably similar to the distribution pattern for the entire American population. Most private schools are not exclusively for the rich. Thus, one cannot simplistically assert that private schools skim the cream of the student pool and leave the public schools only for students from low-income families. In fact, many urban private schools enrol higher proportions of students from low socio-economic-status families than many prestigious suburban public schools.

Now, we can proceed to discuss the formal hypothesis that delinquency rates increase as the proportion of public school students to private school students rises. Some of the rationale underlying this hypothesis – in other words why (unlike the Utilitarians) we might expect that private schools would improve discipline – can be outlined as follows. Private schools provide families and students with a far greater variety of choices than can be found among public schools: there will be choice among different schools per se, and also choice among schools wedded to different programmatic philosophies. For instance, parents may adopt one or another religious affiliation, or choose among schools with the same affiliation but with different administrative styles, or choose between secular (private) or religious schools. This variety should permit parents and students to select a school particularly appropriate to their family needs, or even to shift their choice if their first decision turns out to be unwise. Presumably student discipline should improve as the congruence grows among family, student and school values.

Again, if there is reasonably effective competition (as there may be among private schools), schools that cannot maintain good discipline will suffer a loss of parental support – unless they change. To offer a concrete example of the effect of such competition, recall the well-publicised 'free schools' (many of which were secular private schools) of the late 1960s and early 1970s. At this time, they are practically extinct – they have died because parents stopped patronising them. Conversely, a variety of questionable public school 'innovations' of that same period have died much more slowly than did the free schools – precisely because they were shielded from market forces.

To consider another element of our underlying rationale, recall that the NIE study found that *academic* competition inside school appears to reduce a school's risk of violence. 'The data suggests that violent students are more likely to be those who have given up on school, do not care about grades, find the courses irrelevant, and feel nothing they do makes any difference.' This finding is relevant to the public/private debate. As the NIE report observed, in the 'progressive' atmosphere of modern public school teaching grading has, on average, become de-emphasised because of the preference for 'cooperation over competition'. Private schools in contrast have, on the whole, maintained competition and grading as essential features in education. Consider also the NIE's finding that larger schools experience more violence and vandalism than smaller ones. Private schools in the USA tend to be smaller in terms of pupil enrolment than public schools. For this reason also we should find that private school areas are less crime prone. Incidentally, there is evidence that the steady trend towards larger public schools has been stimulated by the school consolidation movement, a movement led largely by administrators whose own salaries increase as their schools enlarge.[2] The private school system does not lend itself to this kind of push towards monolithic institutions.

If, finally, the data does show that the users of private schools are less crime prone, it would carry with it the strong suggestion that religious schooling is more conducive than public schooling to an orderly society, since 80 per cent of the private schools in the USA are Church-affiliated.

The statistical test

One attempt has already been made at the sort of statistical hypothesis-testing suggested here. In a recent paper, John R. Lott and Gertrud M. Fremling (1980) statistically compared changes in (a) the reported United States national juvenile delinquency rate from 1961 to 1971 to (b) changes in the national proportion of children attending public as compared to private schools. During this period, the national rate of delinquency did, in fact, increase, while the proportion of private school attendees declined (probably largely due to the decline in enrolment in Catholic schools).

Of course, other factors that might affect juvenile delinquency

---

2   Robert Staaf, 'The Public School System in Transition', in T. C. Boreherding (ed.), *Budgets and Bureaucrats*, Duke University Press, Durham, NC, 1977.

such as unemployment and the degree of urbanisation were changing over the same period. But Lott and Fremling used multiple regression analyses which made allowances for these other influences. Their analyses produced statistically significant and robust findings that the expansion in public (relative to private) education during the period studied was associated with consistent increases in delinquency. Thus, during the period, the juvenile delinquency rate increased by 14.8 per thousand, while the number of children attending public schools rose 3.56 per cent. The shift in schools accounted for 22 per cent of the entire increase in delinquency. The remaining 78 per cent of the increase was explained by the other variables examined.

Lott and Fremling deny that their findings are affected by differences in the socio-economic status (SES) of the public and private school pupils, because their study relied on time series analysis. This technique can be explained as follows: in any year, it is possible that private schools (if they were generally filled with higher SES students) might show better discipline than public schools precisely because of their SES advantage. But the data shows that when private school enrolment comparatively declines, and that other factors, such as prosperity, stay constant, there is some steady rise in delinquency. This demonstrates that delinquency is more a function of the type of school than its students' SES. In any case, it is a fact (although Lott and Fremling do not seem to have recognised it) that private schools, as already noted, are *not* the exclusive haven of the rich.

The significant work of Lott and Fremling leads us to the conclusion that, so far, the best research available rebuts the arguments of the Utilitarians and their American equivalents. Public schools – as compared to private schools – do not tend to reduce crime. There is even tentative evidence of reverse causality: juvenile crime actually increases with an increase in size of the public school sector. Incidentally, we should note that this tentative scientific conclusion is widely supported by the opinions and actions of many parents – who obviously believe that private school education is more effective than public along a wide spectrum of outcomes.

The research just discussed will – and should – provoke further study. The issues are not definitively settled. But, if further research confirms that of Lott and Fremling, we must conclude that the costs of public education are much higher than was originally believed. Already published figures show that the *conventional* economic cost of public education is about twice that of private schools.

It now seems as though there may be an argument for adding to that cost the higher social cost of delinquency, even though one of the aims of public schooling has been to lower it.

References

Lott, John R., and Gertrud M. Fremling, *Juvenile Delinquency and Education: An Econometric Study*, International Institute for Economic Research, Westwood Center, Los Angeles, CA, 1980.

West, E. G., *Education and the Industrial Revolution*, Batsford, London, 1975.

7 PUBLIC EDUCATION AND IMPERFECT DEMOCRACY

E. G. West[1]

Introduction

Tibor Machan[2] refers to the paradox wherein a country aspiring to be a fully free society tolerates the continuation of a coercive education system. The system is coercive because (a) it is funded, not by parental payments at the door of the school, but by mandatory taxes that are collected prior to the schooling, (b) students are legally forced to attend, and (c) the choice of school is severely constrained. In Tibor Machan's words, 'the paradox is that, despite all the negatives, folks have become very accustomed to public schools'. I shall attempt to explain why public school systems invariably meet with the success so far indicated, or, in other words, why radical reform seems currently to have only doubtful prospects. A brief initial focus will be on common historical origins of public government schooling worldwide. This will be followed by a critical examination of the present situation from the standpoint of political economy and some assessment of prevailing economic analysis of the current roles of public and private education.

---

1   Reprinted from *Education in a Free Society*, ed. Tibor R. Machan, with the permission of the publisher, Hoover Institution Press. Copyright 2000 by the Board of Trustees of the Leland Stanford Junior University.

2   'Public Education and Its Pitfalls', *Education in a Free Society*, op. cit.

The universal pattern of evolution

In attempting to determine how, over 150 years, we still possess a monopoly public school system that provides a 'one size fits all' education,[3] we shall start with a mental experiment. Consider an initial scenario in which education, like food, is being adequately demanded and supplied via an efficient private sector. How could ambitious politicians or administrators persuade government to intervene in the sense of obtaining for them a threshold of power? One can hypothesise at least two available methods. First, the potential interveners might produce plausible (even if erroneous) statistics showing areas of numerically deficient school attendance. The second method involves a call for respect for the 'proper' boundaries of education and the exclusion of institutions that do not meet the officially approved definition of schooling. Such action will, of course, necessitate a full-time government department and an appropriate number of career civil servants and inspectors.[4]

Statistics of educational need: the case of New York

The history of American education clearly demonstrates the two methods of intervention just described. In 1804 an act was passed providing that the net proceeds of the sale of 500,000 acres of the vacant lands owned by New York State be appropriated as a permanent fund (about $50,000 in value) for the support of schools.

---

3   The phrase 'one size fits all' is something of an exaggeration because the 'size' of public education in wealthy areas of the public system is usually bigger than elsewhere. But the phrase does give a correct impression in terms of mechanical uniformity of practice.

4   Jeremy Bentham and John Stuart Mill adopted both methods in advancing their strong criticisms of nineteenth-century British denominational instruction (West, 1992: 598).

But how much support was actually needed? The answer lay in facts that had not yet been ascertained. To rectify this situation five commissioners were authorised in 1811 to report on a system for the establishment and organisation of Common Schools. Their report appeared in 1812, accompanied by the draft of a bill that was the basis of the act passed later that year. It is interesting to compare the terms of the bill with the rationale of state aid as argued in the report.[5] The commissioners acknowledged that, for state aid to be completely justified, it was necessary to establish in what respects the people were not already securing sufficient education for their children. They conceded immediately that schooling was indeed already widespread: 'In a free government, where political equality is established, and where the road to preferment is open to all, there is a natural stimulus to education; and accordingly *we find it generally resorted to, unless some great local impediments interfere.*'[6]

Poverty was in some cases an impediment; but the biggest obstacle was bad geographic location:

> In populous cities, and the parts of the country thickly settled, *schools are generally established by individual exertion* … It is in the remote and thinly populated parts of the State, where the inhabitants are scattered over a large extent, that education stands greatly in need of encouragement. The people here living far from each other, makes it difficult so to establish schools as to render them convenient or accessible to all. Every family therefore, must either educate its own children, or the children must forgo the advantages of education.[7]

5   J. Randall, *History of the Common School System of the State of New York*, Ivison, Blakeman, Taylor & Co., 1871, p. 18.

6   Ibid., p. 18, my italics.

7   Ibid., my italics.

The problem was thus presented in the same terms as those later to be used in England by W. E. Forster, the architect of the 1870 English Education Act; it was largely a problem, to use Forster's words, of 'filling up the gaps'. The logic of such argument, of course, called mainly for discriminating and marginal government intervention. To this end three policies were available. First, the government could assist families, but only the needy ones, by way of educational subsidies. Second, it could subsidise the promoters of schools in the special areas where they were needed. Third, the government itself could set up schools, but only in the rural 'gap' areas. Without discussing possible alternatives, however, the commissioners promptly recommended that the inconveniences could generally best be remedied 'by the establishment of Common Schools, under the direction and patronage of the State'.

Thus, in place of discrimination in favour of poor and thinly populated districts, a flat equality of treatment was decreed for *all* areas; the public monies were to be distributed on a per capita basis according to the number of children between five and fifteen in each district, whether its population was dense or sparse. Beyond this, each town, at its own discretion, was to raise by tax, annually, as much money as it received from the school fund. It appears, therefore, that what the commissioners had succeeded in doing was guaranteeing, not the education of the most needy, but the emergence of an officially approved 'nationalised' or 'collectivised' education for rich and poor alike and in schools of homogeneous quality. Tibor Machan's complaint about the 'one size fits all' approach to education has thus (in the case of New York) been traced to its origins.

Required conformity with American government definitions of 'education'

As previously explained, the second method of intervention was to throw doubt on the quality of non-public education and to urge an *official* definition of 'proper instruction'. On the whole it was this stratagem which most dominated events in America because, in contrast to Britain, New York State in the early nineteenth century bore fairly clear statistical testimony to the fact that schooling was already widespread. The bureaucracies in this particular state, therefore, avoided the need for the misleading arithmetic being used in Britain which exaggerated the extent of educational negligence (West, 1992: 603–9). Other kinds of forces, however, began inexorably to increase the relative strength of the public over the private school system. American public education was soon being called upon, not primarily, as in Britain, to produce a literate and fully employed population, but instead to condition young people to be independent of their families and to pursue the welfare not of individuals, but of the 'nation'. In so doing, the declared intention was to abolish all aspects of alleged inequity. Students from different backgrounds would be educated in 'common' schools that produced 'social cohesion'. And one of the associated functions of the schools, of course, was to 'Americanise', if not homogenise, new immigrants from Europe.

Prominent in inculcating this new philosophy was Horace Mann, who, in 1837, became the first secretary of the Massachusetts Board of Education. As Sheldon Richman observes: 'For Mann, equalization and social harmony would be advanced by the compulsory mixing of children from rich and poor families' (Richman, 1995: 49). Clearly the existence of private schools that did not share such a philosophy was an obstacle that, for Mann and his followers, had to be overcome.

A new government 'weapon' was accordingly introduced into the struggle. Up to the 1860s parents using the public schools had been obliged to pay 'rate bills' that amounted in financial terms to the equivalent of school fees. Under the Free Schools Act of 1867, however, the rate bills (fees) were abolished. This legislation had the desired result as far as the expanding public education bureaucracy was concerned. It consisted of the marginal 'crowding out' of the private by the public sector. This occurred because when government schools are financed from tax funds and fees are abolished therein, the private sector cannot match the public action. In current terminology there was no longer 'a level playing field'.

Elementary economics predicts that artificial reduction of prices to zero leads to an erosion of appropriate incentives. Bearing in mind the growing monopoly status of the public schools, their administrators disliked one particular degree of freedom that had been left to dissatisfied parents. When the perceived quality of their schooling fell below a given level they could often transfer their older children to non-formal schooling such as training on the job. Predictably the public education elites began to condemn such a 'safety valve' and to demand laws for compulsory schooling. When governments take such action they are, of course, forced to *define* education. In practice this coincided with the type of education being supplied in conventional or standardised public schools. Other types were usually firmly ruled out.

This account of the emergence of compulsion again appears to explain in large part what has been the subsequent emergence of the 'one size fits all' public education that so offends Tibor Machan and others today. The agitation by the teachers' association (and other interest groups) for compulsory laws, following the victory in 1867 of their Free School Campaign, was soon rewarded. The Compulsory Education Act was passed in 1874. And, interestingly enough, after several years of operation, it was declared ineffective. The Superintendent of 1890, asking for yet more legislation, complained that the existing laws were still not reaching the hard core of truant cases, those associated with dissolute families. But even this 'hard core' was conceded to consist of a small minority. It is worse than futile to assume that all persons charged with the care of children will send them to school. The great majority will.[8]

Whatever the fate of the children of the 'hard-case' families, the final link in the process of monopolising had now been firmly secured with respect to the education of all the other children, those in the vast majority of families that were admitted to be fully responsible. Compulsory payment and compulsory consumption had become mutually strengthening monopoly bonds, and the pattern of schooling for the next century had been firmly set.

Pockets of current resistance

Sheldon Richman (1995: 2) observes: 'The public schools, despite their widely recognized problems, [today] have a mystique that prevents people from imagining a life without them.' Questioning them, indeed, has come to be seen by some as audacious, if not irreverent. Yet others believe that the system 'has been an insidious assault on the integrity of the family' (Richman, 1995: 7). Has public education for the bulk of the population become a

---

8   36th Ann. Rep. N.Y. Supt. Public Instruction, 1890, p. 35.

'necessary' institution simply because it is one of those institutions to which people have become accustomed? Whatever the case the relevant bureaucracies have used their overwhelming influence to maintain the system and the status quo.

The power of today's government school bureaucracy can be measured partly by the level of current public education expenditure. With this at over $316 billion, education is now the second-largest entitlement programme in the United States (and the world), ranking behind social security but ahead of Medicare/Medicaid.[9] With money of this magnitude there is presumably more than enough for the public education system for self-advertisement and PR programmemes, together with formidable campaign power to resist all kinds of parental choice proposals. The power and influence of the public system, meanwhile, extend to teacher training schools and education departments of universities, where most authors of histories of education are to be found. If we are to achieve a full understanding of events, however, we must usually put aside the standard histories, which in the words of Mark Blaug 'seem to have been largely written to prove that education is only adequately provided when the state [government] accepts its responsibility to furnish compulsory education *gratis*' (Blaug, 1975: 594).

Official attempts at rationalising the system

The favourite approach of public school advocates in attempting to rationalise the current public system is to assert that it is a crucial component of democracy. It is also urged that it is one that

---

9 Cardiff, 1996.

gives unique protection to the children of the poor. Such claims, however, are more expressions of faith than rationally argued and empirically demonstrated positions. To achieve the latter, the advocates need to address at least the following six questions:

1. If children's education needs the special protection of democracy, why do we not have similar protection in other areas such as government provision of free food, clothing and shelter for children?

2. If parents are allowed to spend from their income directly on their child's food, why, in the case of schooling, is part of that income pre-empted by taxation to provide the *indirect* purchase of 'free' schooling?

3. Again, if parents are allowed the opportunity to give their children immediate protection from inferior food supply by promptly transferring their money and custom from the inefficient store to a better one, why are they not allowed parallel powers to protect the education of their children?

4. How can one argue that democratic provision is necessary for promoting equality of opportunity for the poor when, by preventing their families in downtown ghetto schools from escaping from bad schools, it perpetuates, if not aggravates, inequality of opportunity?

5. Why is it that the choice system that exists within the present system of heterogeneous public schools is available almost exclusively for the middle class and the rich? It is summarised by the words 'buy a house, buy a school'.

6. Finally, while democracy is a simple *majority* voting institution, how can we expect the poor, who constitute a *minority*, to be particularly well served?

The unions

Another pertinent feature of democracy is the presence of alliances between governments (or political parties) and interest groups. In public education the foremost example is the teacher union. While the sternest critics go so far as to complain that government schools are increasingly run by the unions and for the unions, it is important first to analyse one of the most critical areas: that of collective bargaining. When looking for consistency in applying the principles of democracy (or rule by consent), one major factor that emerges is that, in practice, 'collective bargaining in public education constitutes the negotiation of public policies with a special interest group [the union], in a process from which others are excluded. This is contrary to the way public policy should be made in a democratic representative system of government' (Lieberman, 1997: 64). As one conspicuous example, the *Chicago Tribune* has observed that the Chicago Teachers Association now has 'as much control over operations of the public schools as the Chicago Board of Education ... more control than is available to principals, parents, taxpayers, and voters'. The *Tribune* claimed that curriculum matters, for instance, such as programmes for teaching children to read, were written into the (union) contract. Indeed, the board was required to bring *any* proposed changes to the bargaining table (Bovard, 1996: 498).

The leading unions in the USA, NEA and AFT, are strongly opposed to any policy that would introduce competition or would shrink the market for teacher services. 'Thus the NEA/AFT oppose vouchers, tuition tax credits, contracting out, home schooling, or lowering the compulsory age limit for education ... [and] are as adamantly opposed to trial projects or demonstration projects as they are to large scale programmes to allow competition in the education industry' (Lieberman, 1997: 5). It should be noted that such opposition to the programmes described coincides with the strategies that any monopoly would adopt. Observers have to decide, therefore, whether the unions' motive is the latter, or whether their education philosophy derives primarily from pursuit of the 'public interest'.

Simple majority democracies are associated with complex coalitions, large campaign fund accumulations and considerable vote trading. The ability of well-organised and concentrated institutions to 'deliver' vote support is, of course, a very attractive propensity to politicians. The NEA and the AFT are prominent examples. It was in 1972 that the NEA organised its first political action committee (PAC), and by 1992 it was contributing over $2 million to congressional candidates. An additional $2 million, meanwhile, was going to state and national political parties for voter registration and related activities. In the opinion of Lieberman, while the unions do on occasion support Republicans, 'for the most practical purposes, however, the NEA (and AFT) are adjuncts of the Democratic Party' (Lieberman, 1997: 76).

One final aspect of the workings of democracy needs explanation because it is invariably neglected. Specialists in the 'economics of politics' observe that, in single-issue situations, the outcome of voting is determined by the median voter. Consider the following very simple example of a population of five individuals with income distributions shown in Table 2.

If each individual has a vote, then person number 3 is the median voter because there is an equal number of voters on either side of him. Assume that preferences for tax-funded education are distributed in proportion to income. Consider the median voter's preference to be *m*. Voters 4 and 5 will favour *m* over any proposal

Table 2   **Income distribution and the median voter**

Individual income	Case A income, $	Case B income, $
1	1,000	1,000
2	2,000	2,000
3	3,000	3,000
4	4,000	4,000
5	5,000	10,000
Total income	15,000	20,000
Average income	3,000	4,000
Median income	3,000	3,000
Total proceeds of an education tax of 10 per cent of total income	1,500	2,000

to supply less. Voters 2 and 1 will favour it over proposals to supply more. Thus the median voter's preference dominates.

In Table 2 the median voter's income in case A is $3,000, and this is also the average income. Case B, in contrast, shows a 'skewed' income distribution. The presence of exceptionally rich individual number 5 (with income of $10,000) increases the average income to $4,000. This is now $1,000 above the median income (which remains at $3,000). In the real world, income distributions are similarly skewed, although not as 'severely'.

Assume now that public education is financed by a flat tax equal to 10 per cent of income and that education costs $1 per unit. The median voter's education tax in scenario A would be $300, as would that of every other individual (since, to reiterate, the median voter's preference would dominate). The total education tax proceeds in case A therefore would be $300 x 5 = $1,500. Each individual would obtain 300 units of education (bearing in mind that the assumed 'tax price' or cost is $1 per unit).

Next suppose that the scenario changes from A to B. The total and average income increase to $20,000 and $4,000 respectively. The 10 per cent education tax would now generate a total of

$2,000. This would allow the median voter to increase his demanded *quantity* of education to 400 units while still paying $300 in tax. In effect this is a drop in the median voter's tax price per unit of education. Because this 'privilege' is available only through a tax-funded public education system, the median voter will, to that extent, be biased against any proposal to abolish it.

Alternatively, suppose that individual number 5 in Table 2 was initially forfeiting a 'free' public education for his child and instead was patronising a fee-paying private school (i.e. he was 'paying twice' for his education). The total tax revenue available for public education would remain at $2,000. Spread now among only four users of public education, this would amount to an education worth $500 each. Consider next the probable response to a proposal to offer all parents, including those currently using private schooling, an education voucher worth $400 each. The median voter would clearly reject such a 'universal voucher' because he would now be obliged to share the available total of education tax revenue with the rich individual (number 5). The conclusion is that, at least with such elementary models of politics, the forces of democracy would tend to resist such reforms as vouchers.

Several critics of the public school system reject vouchers as a 'solution' anyway because they foresee the future imposition of such a raft of regulatory standards that the recipient schools would become virtually indistinguishable from public schools. But even if one sides with these critics it is necessary to appreciate that the above logic predicts an inherent resistance of the median voter public school supporter to most other 'solutions', including tax credits, contracting out, home schooling and lowering the compulsory age limit for education. Thus the typical concurrence in democracies of positively skewed income distributions, median voter dominance in single-issue situations, and the existence of some fee-paying private schooling leads to the conclusion that the median voter is, to a large extent, grid-locked into the present public school system.

Conclusion

The first part of this essay explored, in historical terms, the evolution of the public education system as we know it today. Desiring to place the system in the arena of politics, ambitious opportunists in the nineteenth century used two approaches. The first was the brandishing of statistics claiming serious educational deficiency, a method that was used especially in Britain. The second method, used more especially in America under such leaders as Horace Mann, was to condemn the nature and content of the hitherto flourishing private schooling. It was now insisted that private schools were not in a position to offer the 'true' kind of education.

No apology is made for the brief historical account at the beginning of this essay because we can now see history repeating itself in the reappearance of such arguments. According to one specialist in the child care area, advocates of increased government involvement in this field 'generally argue that (1) there is a shortage of child care facilities, (2) unregulated child care is harmful to children'.[10] As we have seen, these are precisely the two types of argument that proved so successful in obtaining government intervention in the nineteenth century. According to my analysis of the latter situation, the empirical evidence did not support the offered rationale. Apparently (see Olsen, 1997) the same is true today.

---

10   Olsen, 1997: 1.

Staunch supporters of the current public school system attempt to rationalise it via a series of further a priori arguments. A leading one is the assertion that public schools have become necessary institutions because they are an essential part of democracy. Our essay, however, has posed six questions that tend to challenge this assumption on its own grounds. Beyond this, a full description of democracy calls for a proper investigation of government alliances in the real world with interest groups such as teacher unions. As conducted today, it has been maintained that these institutions are often serious *obstacles* to democracy.

References

Annual 19th Century Reports of New York Superintendents of Public Instruction.

Becker, Gary S. (1995), 'Human Capital and Poverty Alleviation', HRO Working Paper, World Bank, March.

Blaug, Mark (1975), 'The Economics of Education in English Classical Political Economy: A Re-examination', in A. Skinner and T. Wilson, *Essays on Adam Smith*, Clarendon Press, Oxford, p. 595.

Bovard, James (1996), 'Teachers' Unions: Are the Schools Run for Them?', *The Freeman*, July.

Cardiff, Chris (1996), 'Education: What about the Poor?', *The Freeman*, July.

Epple, Dennis, and Richard Romano (1998), 'Educational Vouchers and Cream Skimming', Carnegie Mellon University Working Paper.

Friedman, Milton (1962), *Capitalism and Freedom*, University of Chicago Press.

Friedman, Milton and Rose (1980), *Free to Choose*, Harcourt Brace Jovanovich, New York.

Lieberman, Myron (1997), *The Teacher Unions*, Free Press, New York.

Lowe, Robert (1868), *Middle Class Education: Endowment or Free Trade?*, Bush, London.

Lyman, Isabel (1998), *Home Schooling: Back to the Future?*, Policy Analysis no. 294, CATO Institute, Washington, DC.

Manski, Charles F. (1992), 'Educational Choice (Vouchers) and Social Mobility', *Economics of Education Review* 11(4): 351–69.

McGroaty, D. (1994), 'School Choice Slandered', *Public Interest* 117: 94–111.

Nechyba, Thomas J. (1998), 'Mobility and Private School Vouchers', Department of Economics Working Paper, Stanford University, CT.

Olsen, Darcy (1997), 'The Advancing Nanny State', *Policy Analysis* 285, CATO Institute, October.

Randall, J. (1871), *History of the Common School System of the State of New York*, Ivison, Blakeman, Taylor & Co., p. 18.

Richman, Sheldon (1995), *Separating School and State*, Future of Freedom Foundation, Fairfax, VA.

Rouse, C. E. (1996), 'Private School Vouchers and Student Achievement: An Evaluation of the Milwaukee Parental Choice Program', Working Paper no. 371, Industrial Relations Section, Princeton University, NJ.

Toma, Eugenia F. (1999), 'Will Johnny Read Next Year?', 15th Annual Lecture in the Virginia Political Economy Lecture Series, 18 March.

West, Edwin G. (1975), *Nonpublic School Aid*, Lexington Books.

West, Edwin G. (1992), 'The Benthamites as Educational

Engineers', *History of Political Economy* 24: 3.

West, Edwin G. (1994), *Education and the State*, Institute of Economic Affairs, London, 1965; 2nd edn, 1970; 3rd edn (revised and extended), Liberty Fund, Indianapolis, IN, 1994.

8 TOM PAINE'S VOUCHER SCHEME FOR PUBLIC EDUCATION

E. G. West[1]

The classical economists, as is commonly known, were in favour of appreciable government intervention in English education.[2] Their arguments were based on the conviction that large numbers of families, if unaided, would seriously under-invest in education. This conviction was based on two simple observations: first, that many parents were too poor to buy education; second, that many others did not sufficiently value it. Such reasoning led some of these writers to advocate compulsory laws. It is especially interesting to note also that it led them to propose government subsidies to the schools rather than directly to the scholars (or their parents). The purpose of this essay is to draw attention to, and to analyse, the proposals of a contemporary of the classical economists, who also wanted more education but who advocated quite a different means. Believing that the majority of poor people were much more aware of the benefits of education than was commonly supposed, and contending that it was heavy taxation of the masses which was the chief cause of their poverty, this writer made

---

1   This essay originally appeared in the *Southern Economic Journal* 3(3), January 1967, and is reprinted by kind permission of the Southern Economic Association.

2   For further details, see E. G. West, 'Private versus Public Education: A Classical Economic Dispute', *Journal of Political Economy*, October 1964; West, *Education and the State*, Institute of Economic Affairs, London, 1965, ch. 8; William L. Miller, 'The Economics of Education in English Classical Economics', *Southern Economic Journal*, January 1966, pp. 294–309.

particularly interesting and original fiscal suggestions to promote education which seem hitherto to have been neglected by historians of economic thought.

The widespread incidence of poverty at the end of the eighteenth and the first half of the nineteenth centuries was a powerful factor which influenced nearly all the classical economists in their advocacy of state-aided education. But it is at first sight surprising that in the context of education they did not so readily associate parental poverty with the prevailing heavy burden of taxation. It is often forgotten that the bulk of the central revenue in those days came from indirect taxes, most of which were strongly regressive. Taxes on food and tobacco, for instance, typically accounted for about 60 per cent of all central revenue in the first half of the nineteenth century. In addition, the independent poor were obliged to pay increasingly burdensome poor rate levies, particularly after 1800. Lack of clarity or sophistication concerning the true incidence of taxation, together with a certain moral asceticism in favour of taxing some 'unnecessaries', provide two explanations of the attitude of several of the early economists. Adam Smith's view was that taxes on the necessities of the poor were all passed on to the employers in the form of higher wages. J. R. McCulloch objected to income tax, proposals for which were being increasingly pressed after 1820, on the grounds of the difficulty of making individual assessments. He was even more critical of the principle of graduation because he thought it would have uncontrollable redistributional consequences.[3]

In practice, contemporary governments had become habitually accustomed to enormous revenues from taxes on necessaries

---

3   See J. R. McCulloch, *Treatise on the Principles and Practical Influence of Taxation*, 1845, pp. 7, 42, 119–26.

and looked upon them 'as of right'. Once the revenues from the indirect taxes had been collected, it was certainly difficult to claim that the poor deserved to be refunded. For, as many economists emphasised, there were certain benefits that the government supplied, such as defence, which were indivisible and enjoyed by all and so were regarded as deserving of a contribution from all. Propositions for a *new* universal government service in aid of the poor to be provided *ex ante* from *new* levies specifically for that purpose would have been open to clearer debate. If, for instance, the new levies could have been shown to be expected to fall mainly on the poor themselves, then the policy would have been more clearly seen as one of paternalism rather than one of redistribution. The appropriateness of such a policy could then have been discussed more directly in the light of evidence on the responsibility of the average poor in spending their own money.

However, as so often when decisions were proposed or actually made through the political process, demand choices became arbitrarily separated from supply choices. Thus in educational policy, as in many other fields, the tendency was for schemes to be pushed in advance of the determination of the requisite finance. In the nineteenth century, when incomes were rising, governments were typically enabled to find the finance for particular measures after the event of legislation. Their path was made easier by virtue of what Gladstone called the 'buoyancy of the revenue'. Because of this constant syphoning process upon gradually rising incomes, poor families were prevented from having as much disposable income as they would otherwise have enjoyed. It is not at all clear that, had taxation been restrained and disposable incomes increased, *average* families would not have used the difference to buy much more education directly. An educational threshold had directly been reached by very large numbers of ordinary people. James Mill, for instance, observed in 1813:

> From observation and inquiry assiduously directed to that object, we can ourselves speak decidedly as to the rapid progress which the love of education is making among the lower orders in England. Even around London, in a circle of fifty miles radius, which is far from the most instructed and virtuous part of the kingdom, there is hardly a village that has not something of a school; and not many children of either sex who are not taught more or less, reading and writing. We have met with families in which, for weeks together, not an article of sustenance but potatoes had been used; yet for every child the hard-earned sum was provided to send them to school.[4]

Considering the number of adherents of the 'ability to pay principle' in public finance, adherents such as J. S. Mill and his followers, it is surprising that the movement for more equity in nineteenth-century taxation was not more vociferous than it was.[5] It has often been observed, however, that in the early nineteenth century there were formidable administrative obstacles hindering such reform. The common view is that the principle of equity is effected much more easily and accurately through a system of income tax allowances. Furthermore, and especially in view of the

---

4   James Mill, *Edinburgh Review*, February 1813; reprinted in West, *Education and the State*, op. cit., ch. 10, p. 136.

5   J. S. Mill recognised the principle thus: 'The principle, therefore, of equality of taxation, interpreted in its only just sense, equality of sacrifice, requires that a person who has no means of providing for old age, or for *those in whom he is interested*, except by saving from income, should have the tax remitted on all that part of his income which is really and *bona fide* applied to that purpose.' *Principles of Political Economy*, Ashley edn, 1915, p. 813 (emphasis added).

argument that, in education, there is a strong case for financial contributions from non-parents, some modern writers would point to the necessity of a negative income tax over some range of income. Income tax, however, had hardly begun in the nineteenth century. Nevertheless, there was one contemporary writer who did attempt to show the feasibility of such sophistication and discrimination even within the framework of an indirect tax system. His work as an economist has suffered neglect owing partly no doubt to the extent to which his political views embarrassed other economists and indeed the country at large. He was none other than Tom Paine.[6]

At the end of his notorious work *The Rights of Man*, Paine made a review of the current taxation situation. He first examined the contention that there was an inexorable law that taxes increased with the passage of time. This he condemned as fatalistic. Quoting Sir John Sinclair's *History of the Revenue*, he showed that the English people had succeeded in getting their taxes continually *reduced* for the four hundred years starting from 1066. At the expiration of this time they were reduced by three-fourths, viz. from £400,000 to £100,000 in 1466. Since that time, however, the taxes had risen so much that Paine thought the national character of the English had weakened. For in 1791 taxation amounted to £17,000,000. The main increases, said Paine, were associated with war years, which gave rise to an enlargement of the national debt.[7]

The composition of taxes in 1788 was as shown in Table 3.

Between 1788 and 1791, therefore, taxes had risen by one and a half million pounds. The land tax, paid by the aristocrats, was the

---

6   Smith and Malthus openly denounced his political writings.

7   A thesis since developed by A. Peacock and J. Wiseman, *The Growth of Public Expenditure in the United Kingdom*, Oxford University Press, 1961.

Table 3   **Composition of taxes in 1788**

	£
Land tax	1,950,000
Customs	3,789,274
Excise (including old and new malt)	6,751,727
Stamps	1,278,214
Miscellaneous taxes and incidents	1,803,755
Total	15,572,970

only one that was falling, having dropped by half a million pounds over the previous century.[8]

Nine million of the total revenue was applied to servicing the national debt, the remaining eight million went on current expenses. It was the latter which Paine thought to be extravagant.[9] Independently of all this, the cost of administering poor relief, which amounted to two million, was largely escaped by the rich.

Paine gave several reasons as to why the ordinary current expenses of eight million could be reduced to one and a half million. But the question then arose of how to dispose of the surplus of over six million. Reducing the excise would be a step in the right direction, but there was need for a nicer discrimination within the group that paid it. He looked next to the reduction of other taxes: 'where the relief will be direct and visible, and capable of immediate operation'.[10] The poor rates, he said, were a direct tax, 'which every housekeeper feels and who knows also, to a farthing, the sum

8   The aristocrats also avoided the beer tax because home-brewed ale did not attract duty, and they alone brewed it in large enough quantities to make it economic. The proceeds of the beer tax exceeded that of the land tax.

9   With regard to the interest and the national debt, he thought it was heavy: 'yet as it serves to keep alive a capital useful to commerce, it balances by its effects a considerable part of its own weight …'

10   Tom Paine, *The Rights of Man*, Everyman edn, London, 1961, ch. 5, p. 245.

he pays'.[11] Furthermore the poor rate, together with other taxation, was the main cause of the poverty itself. Money taken in taxation from average families was much more than enough to finance a basic education of their children. A labouring man with a wife and two or three children paid between seven and eight pounds a year in taxes. 'He is not sensible of this, because it is disguised to him in the articles which he buys, and he thinks only of their dearness; but as the taxes take from him, at least, *a fourth of his yearly earnings*, he is consequently disabled from providing for a family, especially if himself or any of them are afflicted with sickness.'[12]

Paine, the son of a weaver, had a great respect for the good sense of average parents and, of all institutions, that of the family was to his mind the most noble. His own experience led him to value the moral instruction by his own father.[13] He objected to the impartial effects of the taxes: 'Speaking for myself, my parents were not able to give me a shilling beyond what they gave me in education; and to do this they distressed themselves.'[14] Paine argued that small householders were more injured by the taxes than others just because they consumed more of the taxable articles, in proportion to their property, than those with large estates, and second, their residences were chiefly in towns, where the poor rates were more severe.

It was easily seen, said Paine, that the bulk of the really poor consisted of two groups: first, large families of children; second, old people. Equity demanded therefore that the surplus should

---

11   Ibid. The 'poor rates' were taxes assessed on property for local support of the poor and indigent.

12   Ibid., p.246 (emphasis added).

13   In retrospect he preferred the instruction of his father to that of his schoolmaster, who had filled him with 'false heroism'.

14   Ibid., p. 234. His father was a Quaker.

be distributed to these two classes. He proposed in lieu of the poor rates: 'to make a remission of taxes to the poor of double the amount of the present poor rates, viz., four millions annually, out of the surplus taxes. By this measure the poor will be benefited two millions, and the housekeeper two millions.'[15] Moreover, and this is where Paine was even more in advance of his time, the distribution of the surplus four million was to be according to the size and age of the family. Thus he would pay *as a remission of taxes*: '... to every poor family, out of the surplus taxes, and in room of poor rates four pounds a year for every child under fourteen years of age; enjoining the parents of such children to send them to school, to learn reading, writing, and common arithmetic; *the ministers of every parish, of every denomination to certify jointly to an office, for that purpose, that this duty is performed*'.[16]

By a simple statistical estimate, Paine calculated that this education grant would cost approximately two and a half million pounds. This whole operation would, he thought, relieve the poverty of the parents: 'because it is from the expense of bringing up children that their poverty arises'.[17] It would also abolish ignorance and help to set young people on their feet.

Paine was also concerned with the difficulty of inaccessible schooling in sparsely populated areas. To meet this problem, he proposed a special allowance for each child living in these areas. The allowance would amount to ten shillings a year: '... for the expense of schooling for six months each, which would give them

---

15   Ibid., p. 247.

16   Ibid., p. 248 (emphasis added). This suggestion, which seems to share the same basic philosophy as the voucher principle first put forward by Milton Friedman in 1955, published in R. A. Solo, *Economics and the Public Interest.*

17   Ibid.

six months' schooling each year, and half-a-crown a year for paper and spelling books'.[18] He estimated that this would have cost a quarter of a million. He was confident that persons could be found in every village capable and willing to teach, such as distressed clergymen's widows. 'Whatever is given on this account to children answers two purposes; to them it is education – to those who educate them it is a livelihood.'[19] So comprehensively had Paine worked out his scheme that he had not forgotten to consider that ever-important final test of any fiscal scheme – its administrative feasibility. He claimed that his plan was easy in practice: 'It does not embarrass trade by a sudden interruption in the order of taxes, but effects the relief by changing the application of them; and the money necessary for the purpose can be drawn from the excise collections, which are eight times a year in every market town in England.'[20]

Thus, Paine offered a series of fiscal innovations to meet the desire for increased popular education, a desire that the classical economists shared. Paine's scheme distinguished itself from the means proposed by the latter mainly in that it directed the finance not at the school but at the scholar (via his parent or guardian). It will be remembered that Adam Smith argued for a wide dispersal of educational expenditure and decision-making in order to prevent the teacher's rewards from being made independent of his efforts. To this end Smith always wanted some part of education expenses to be paid in the form of fees; the public subsidies that he proposed to be confined mainly to the construction and maintenance of school buildings. But Paine's proposal, judged by

18   Ibid., p. 252.
19   Ibid.
20   Ibid., p. 256.

the criterion of decentralised decision-making, went much farther than that of Smith. For it ensured the possibility of the exercise of a still-wider choice on behalf of the child. Accordingly, still-greater competition would emerge since a much bigger proportion of educational expenditure would go through parental hands.[21]

Again, Paine's scheme was more consistent with J. S. Mill's taxation principle of 'ability to pay'. It also answered the latter's fear that many parents could not be trusted; for parental freedom was joined with the corroborative evidence of a wide selection of local inspectors.[22] Furthermore the dispersion of decision-making was one answer to J. S. Mill's fear that central government control of education would lead to government's 'despotism over the minds' of people. According to Paine, decentralised education would counter the prevailing desire of the aristocrats to maintain their power by depending on ignorance: 'A Nation under a well-regulated Government should permit none to remain uninstructed. It is monarchical and aristocratical Government only that requires ignorance for its support.'[23] Finally, Paine's proposals had the independent aim of abolishing the pernicious effects of the poor law. This in turn was intended to achieve that reduction of crime which most of the classical economists wanted to remove by education alone. For it was Tom Paine's belief that the real

---

21 Paine upheld the principles of commerce with no less vigour than Adam Smith. Thus: 'In all my publications, where the matter would admit, I have been an advocate for commerce, because I am a friend to its effects. It is a pacific system, operating to cordialise mankind, by rendering Nations, as well as individuals, useful to each other. As to the mere theoretical reformation, I have never preached it up. The most effectual process is that of improving the condition of man by means of his interest; and it is on this ground that I take my stand.'

22 i.e. in the shape of the ministers of the parish of every denomination.

23 Paine, op. cit., p. 252.

source of the growth of crime was the demoralising influence of the system of parish relief.

> By the operation of this plan, the poor laws, those instruments of civil torture, will be superseded, and the wasteful expense of litigation prevented. The hearts of the humane will not be shocked by ragged and hungry children, and persons of seventy or eighty years of age, begging for bread. The dying poor will not be dragged from place to place to breathe their last, as a reprisal of parish upon parish. Widows will have maintenance for their children, and not be carted away, on the death of their husbands, like culprits and criminals; and children will no longer be considered as increasingly the distresses of their parents. The haunts of the wretched will be known, because it will be to their advantage, and the number of petty crimes, the offspring of distress and poverty, will be lessened. The poor, as well as the rich, will then be interested in the support of Government, and the cause and apprehension of riots and tumults will cease.[24]

---

24   Ibid., p. 256.

9 EDUCATION VOUCHERS IN PRINCIPLE AND PRACTICE: A SURVEY
E. G. West[1]

An education voucher system exists when governments make payments to families that enable their children to enter public or private schools of their choice. The tax-funded payments can be made directly to parents or indirectly to the selected schools; their purpose is to increase parental choice, to promote school competition, and to allow low-income families access to private schools. Some opponents predict that vouchers will destroy the public system, aggravate poverty, and foster segregation. Others fear that voucher-receiving independent schools will be regulated out of recognition.

The main purpose of this article is to examine the recent emergence of voucher systems as an interesting phenomenon in its own right. The evidence summarised relates to voucher systems operating in twenty countries, provinces, and states. The typical 'funds follow the child' voucher system, in which governments subsidise 'schools of choice' in strict proportion to enrolment, appears to be the favourite form. This type of voucher has been adopted by developing countries – notably Bangladesh, Belize, Chile, Colombia, Guatemala and Lesotho – as well as by industrial countries such as Poland, Sweden, the United Kingdom and the United States.

---

1   This essay originally appeared in the *World Bank Research Observer* 12(1), February 1997, and is reprinted by kind permission of Oxford University Press.

Much of the recorded experience with such programmes is pertinent to the long-standing theoretical debates on the desirability of voucher systems.

A tax-funded education voucher in the broadest sense is a payment made by the government to a school chosen by the parent of the child being educated; the voucher finances all or most of the tuition charged. The system introduces competition among public schools and between public and private schools; and it enables schools to offer diverse educational packages to meet the different preferences of parents.

The voucher systems discussed here apply to education up to and including high school and are funded through tax revenues. First, however, it is important to understand the rationale for the basic intervention that calls upon taxpayers to finance education.

The rationale for state intervention

In economics the three most quoted normative reasons for state intervention in education are to protect children against negligent parents, to internalise beneficial 'externalities', and to ensure equality of opportunity. Compulsory education laws are generally regarded as satisfying the first argument for state intervention. The externalities argument, to be completely persuasive, needs the support of evidence that externalities really exist and are positive at the margin – that is, that people outside the family unit are willing to pay for extra units of education beyond what parents would purchase. In the absence of formal or systematic evidence, most writers simply assume, explicitly or implicitly, that positive marginal external benefits do exist.

The third argument for intervention – the need to ensure

equality of opportunity – reflects concern about the distributional implications of purely private provision. Richer parents are likely to spend more than poorer parents to educate their children, just as they spend more on cars, homes and clothes. The view that children's life chances should not depend on the wealth of their parents or the fortuitous circumstances of the community in which they live is widely accepted. The prospect of upward mobility, of ensuring that one's children will be better off, has been a keystone of political support for the public school system in the past.

This 'equality' argument for intervention depends on the assumption that governments are best equipped to supply the appropriate institutions. But a public system that confines children to schools nearest their home or within administratively determined attendance zones can actually reduce mobility. And where the quality of public education is better in middle-class zones than elsewhere, upward mobility is obviously blocked. In other words, the public system can often narrow a child's options, forcing the child to attend an inferior school when a superior one may be physically within reach. One of the arguments for vouchers is that they enable families to break through these obstacles to give equal opportunity a genuine chance.

The rationale for voucher systems

The goal of all voucher plans – to provide families with maximum choice within a decentralised and competitive system of schools – embodies four principles: consumer choice, personal advancement, the promotion of competition, and equal opportunity. Consumer choice, in education, equals parental choice: parents choose schools for their children by virtue of their parental authority and are thus, in a fundamental sense, the real consumers of education. Under a voucher plan, government serves the consumers of education – parents – rather than the suppliers of education – schools.

The second principle, that of personal advancement, is rooted in the conviction that people want to shape their own destinies. The opportunity to choose and to decide stimulates interest, participation, enthusiasm and dedication. Many government programmes – for example, social security, welfare, health programmes, student loans – directly subsidise the individual recipients with funding for services among which they can select. Social security recipients, for example, can spend their cheques however they choose. The goal of educational vouchers is to extend this principle to education.

The third principle, the stimulation of competition, applies here because public schools are usually monopolies. The objective of vouchers is to challenge them to compete – with each other and with private schools – through reducing costs, increasing quality, and introducing dynamic innovation.

The fourth principle – the goal of equality of opportunity – underlying the rationale for vouchers is a logical outcome of the other three and is expressed in the objective of increasing access to private schools. This goal is embodied particularly in those 'selective', or targeted, voucher schemes that give low-income families greater access to private schools, schemes that have been advocated by Oakland (1994) and Becker (1993). Oakland concludes that a case can be made for some redistribution in the provision of social services generally but suggests that redistribution is better accomplished by extending the welfare system to provide the poor with vouchers for selective government services such as education. This is in preference to the usual system whereby higher levels of government supply lower levels with grants that vary with the levels of local wealth and income. Although fiscal considerations are a factor in Becker's recommendation, he advocates a targeted system primarily 'because the bottom quarter or so of the population are most in need of better education' (p. 11). He quotes studies that not only demonstrate the superior performance of private over public schools in the United States, but also show that 'students from disadvantaged backgrounds tend to gain the most from attending private schools'. This fact, he observes, is not surprising 'in light of the more extensive choices available to middle class and rich students' (p. 12).

Studies comparing the performance of public with private schools in developing countries generally appear to match those in the United States. Analysis, for instance, by Lockheed and Jimenez (1994) of private and public secondary schools in five developing countries revealed that private schools have a significant advantage both in student achievement and in unit costs.

Different applications of the voucher principle

Under most tax-funded voucher systems, education is compulsory up to a legal school leaving age, but parents are free to choose among alternative suppliers of the compulsory service. Compared with an education tax rebate, vouchers help even those who pay little in direct taxation.

With vouchers children are not assigned to schools by attendance zones or any other criterion of the school system. Instead, vouchers enable parents to select a school for their children among any eligible and participating schools, public or private. In the most common application of the voucher principle, known as 'funds follow the child', government funding is directed straight to the school chosen by the parent. Because it has no other direct government subsidy, each school is thus in competition with every other school for students. Good schools attract many students, redeem many vouchers, and prosper. Inferior schools, avoided by parents, are stimulated to improve or must close down.

In practice, tax-funded voucher systems operate under many different regulatory rubrics, which may include government inspection of schools receiving the vouchers. They may also operate only under the condition that the teachers are licensed by the government. Vouchers may be available to all families or to low-income families. The value of the vouchers can also be made to vary inversely with income, so that poorer families receive vouchers worth more than those received by richer families. A variant of the funds-follow-the-child arrangement is a system of chits, given to each parent, cashable only by appropriately designated schools, who then return their vouchers to the relevant government authority and receive the cash value, which they use to pay expenses such as staff salaries. The value of the chit could be equal to, or somewhat less than, per student government expenditure in public schools. Finally, vouchers might provide access to private schools only, public (government) schools only, or to both public and private schools.

Selective vouchers

Selective vouchers can be restricted to families receiving less than a given income level. Such vouchers can, of course, be found outside the context of education. They have been used for housing, for health, and – perhaps the best example for these purposes

– for food, in the United States federal government's food stamp programme. The federal government uses an income test to determine eligibility for food stamps. Recipients use the stamps instead of cash to buy groceries. The grocery stores then return the stamps to the federal government and receive cash in return. This method is similar to the 'chits' version of education vouchers described above. But whereas black market operations seriously threaten the food stamp system, the school voucher largely avoids this problem because it is quite difficult to transfer (sell) the rights to the education obtained.

Selective vouchers can be allocated on the basis of gender as well as income. In Bangladesh, for instance, vouchers are supplied exclusively to females in grades six through ten.

Open enrolment and charter schools

It is sometimes contended that the objectives of vouchers can largely be achieved exclusively within the public sector. This argument involves the so-called 'open enrolment system', wherein the family can choose public schools across extensive geographic areas. In practice, however, disproportionate applications to enrol in a popular school lead administrators to declare it to be full. Unpopular schools, therefore, are not faced with serious costs of under-capacity and typically continue to survive such weak competition.

Another potentially interesting scheme is the relatively new phenomenon of charter schools. These are decentralised and fairly autonomous institutions that operate under contract or charter to an authorised public body. If a charter school does not attract and keep its students, it will go out of business and its charter will be revoked.

Because government subsidises the charter school in direct proportion to its enrolments, the voucher principle is at least partially respected because 'funds follow the child'; for the principle to be fully respected, private schools would also have to be eligible to receive the grants. Nevertheless the charter school provides some alternative to the one public school in a child's administration zone to which he or she is usually assigned. In urban areas, moreover, parents may be able to choose between charter schools themselves.

Voucher systems in operation

Table 4 summarises voucher systems for primary and secondary education that have been implemented in twenty countries, states or provinces around the world in the 1990s. Typically these voucher systems are the funds-follow-the-child kind, in which governments subsidise schools in strict proportion to enrolments.

Space does not allow extended discussion of each entry in Table 4. Five countries have therefore been selected for brief comment here; as case studies they may cast some light on the arguments for and against vouchers reviewed in the next section. The countries are Chile, Colombia, Puerto Rico, the United States (Milwaukee), and the United Kingdom.

Chile

Following the introduction of subsidised ('voucherised') private education in Chile in 1980, the number of students attending private schools increased considerably. By 1988 private schools accommodated 30.4 per cent of the elementary school population

Table 4 **Education vouchers: a cross-country survey of primary and secondary schooling**

Country	Qualifying population	Coverage	Scope of regulations and practices	Monetary value of voucher
Bangladesh	Females, grades 6–10	Selected localities	Public or private schools, minimum attendance and progress required	From $12 in G6 to $36.25 in G10
Chile	Low-income elementary and secondary school attendees	Over one third of total enrolments. All income groups	Receiving schools can also charge fees	Average value in 1991 4,359 pesos
Belize	Elementary and secondary school attendees	75 per cent of primary, 50 per cent of secondary	Strong government partnership with the Churches	n/a
Lesotho	All secondary and primary school attendees	Most schools	Government trains and appoints teachers. Strong partnership with the Churches	n/a
Colombia	Low-income students	Operational in 216 municipalities. Vouchers usable in private schools	Programme participation renewable if student performance satisfactory	$143 per year
Guatemala	Selected low-income girl students between 7 and 14 years old	13 local communities	Minimum attendance and progress required	Approx. $50 per annum
Sweden	All children subject to compulsory education	All municipal areas	Schools must follow national curriculum. Supervision by the National Assembly of Education (NAE)	At least 85 per cent of per pupil cost in municipal schools
The Netherlands	All children subject to compulsory education	All municipal areas	State finance of schools for each religion where local demand demonstrated. Secular private schools also state-financed	Public and private schools are financed on a completely equal basis
Japan	School-children over 15 years old	Public and private high schools	Private schools must submit financial statements to the Foundation for the Promotion of Private Schools	40 per cent of the cost in private high schools covered by government – approximately 140 yen per student in the 1980s
USA (a) tax-funded vouchers	Low-income students in the city of Milwaukee. Maximum 1,500 students	Private non-sectarian schools	Participating schools must limit voucher students to 65 per cent of the student body	$2,900 per year (1994)

USA (b) privately funded vouchers	Low-income families. First come, first served (under the Golden Rule Model)	All reputable non-government schools	Some programmes require parents to match the voucher (scholarship) amount in making tuition payments. No heavy burden on reporting requirements.	Average $6,383 in 1995
Puerto Rico (until 1995)	Families with school-age children and incomes below $18,000	Public and private schools	Use of a lottery when demand for vouchers exceeds supply	$1,500
UK	Low-income students with above-average ability	'Assisted Places' in private schools only	Participating schools must be approved by Education Department	$3,500 (approx.) per year on average (1992)
Poland	Families associated with one of the 36 sponsoring organisations, including the University of Warsaw	Private and mainly non-sectarian schools	Government approval required to open independent schools. A wide variety of curricula allowed in practice	Per capita subsidy level at 50 per cent expenditure
New Zealand	Choice allowed for all school-age children	All public sector schools and selected independent schools	Open enrolment system in a considerably decentralised public sector. School autonomy strengthened via local parent-elected boards	Teacher salary grants to independent schools amounting to 20 per cent in 1993 with expressed intentions to raise it eventually to 50 per cent
Canada: Province of British Columbia	Families patronising independent schools	Denominational and secular private schools	Schools receiving vouchers have to have been established for 3 years minimum	30 per cent of public school costs per student ($500 in 1978)
Canada: Province of Québec	Families patronising independent schools	Mainly private secondary schools	Public inspection. Teachers must have same qualifications as in public schools. Same curriculum	60 per cent of the costs of public schooling (80 per cent for schools 'in the public interest')
Canada: Province of Manitoba	Families patronising independent schools	Private schools	Public inspection	Full-time equivalent capitation grants
Canada: Province of Alberta	Families patronising independent schools	Private schools	Curriculum, teacher qualifications, language requirements	50 per cent of public school cost

Sources: Chile: Winkler and Rounds, 1993; Sweden: OECD, 1994; The Netherlands: OECD, 1994; Japan: Lynn, 1986; USA (Milwaukee): McGroaty, Daniel, 1994; USA (private vouchers): National Scholarship Center, 1995; Puerto Rico: Tucker and Lauber, 1995; UK: UK Department of Education, 1992, World Bank, 1995, Flew, 1995; Poland: Glenn, 1995; New Zealand: OECD, 1994; Canada: Easton, 1988; Bangladesh, Belize, Lesotho, Colombia, Guatemala: World Bank sources.

(compared with 14 per cent in 1980) and 40.8 per cent of total secondary school registration (compared with 15.9 per cent in 1980).

The Chilean reforms were described by the government as a move towards decentralisation. Public schools were transferred to the municipalities, and a new subsidy law provided for the allocation of resources on a per pupil basis and on equal conditions to both private and municipal schools. A 'student performance examination' called Programa de Rendimiento Escolar (PER) operated between 1982 and 1984. This programme lasted only two years because it encountered political difficulties. The Sistema de Mediación de Calidad de Educación (SIMCE) national test followed in 1988. It indicated that the quality of education was significantly higher in the subsidised private educational establishments than in the municipal schools (with the exception of one group). The reforms were followed by an increase in the average number of years of schooling among the Chilean population, including the lower-income groups.

Economic recession has brought some setbacks in recent years, notably a reduction in the real value of the voucher, but to offset this partially the new private schools have been allowed, since 1993, to charge fees for their services. This provision enables parents voluntarily to pay additional sums to their school with the object of trying to maintain or increase educational quality. Municipal primary (elementary) schools are not allowed to charge fees.

Colombia

A voucher system was introduced in 1992 and by 1994 was operating in 216 municipalities, serving 90,807 low-income students in

1,789 schools. The vouchers, worth on average about $143, were issued to students entering the sixth grade. An early examination of the programme confirmed that, as intended, the vouchers were being successfully allocated exclusively to poor families.

The voucher system was introduced primarily to respond to the shortage of places in public secondary schools in Colombia, where 40 per cent of the secondary schools are privately owned. The vouchers help poor students gain access to the private schools; simultaneously, the vouchers benefit the public secondary schools by reducing overcrowding.

The Colombian experience recalls that of Vermont in the United States, where approximately 95 per cent of the state's 246 communities have no public secondary schools. The communities choose instead to pay for their students to attend either private high schools or public high schools in another town. This programme has been in place for more than a century 'to enable small and geographically distant communities around the state to provide high school education for students without incurring the expense of building their own public schools' (Walberg and Bast, 1993: 109).

Puerto Rico

Puerto Rico's governor, Pedro Rosello, signed a voucher plan into law in September 1993, limited to families earning below a given income.

The vouchers, worth $1,500, have been portable between public schools, as well as from private to public and public to private schools; religious schools were also included.

Preliminary evidence appears to refute opponents' predictions that a voucher programme would ruin the public school system. Of the 1,809 vouchers awarded in the autumn of 1993, 1,181 were used by students to transfer from one public school to another, 317 to move from private to public schools, and 311 to shift from public to private schools.

Following opposition and litigation from the teachers' unions, who argued that it was unconstitutional to use vouchers at schools affiliated with religions, the Supreme Court of Puerto Rico ruled on 30 November 1994 (5–2) that the scholarship programme allowing low-income students to attend the school of their choice violated Puerto Rico's constitution. The court, however, permitted the programme to continue until the end of the school year (1995). Meanwhile Governor Rosello and other supporters have promised to try to find a way to continue the programme.

Milwaukee, USA

One of the most striking examples of a successful voucher system for the poor is found in Milwaukee, Wisconsin, in the United States. Pioneered largely by Democrat representative 'Polly' Williams in 1990, the plan originally permitted up to 1,000 low-income students to use state funds ($2,967 for the 1994/5 school year; the amount is adjusted annually) to attend a private, non-sectarian school of their choice.

The Milwaukee programme began operation in 1990 with 300 children using vouchers at six private schools. Five years later (1995) 832 students attended one of eleven participating private schools. The Milwaukee plan has been opposed by various educational establishment groups, including the State School Board Association and the Wisconsin Congress of Parents and Teachers,

Inc. This opposition has probably influenced the administrative restrictions that have accumulated recently. Thus in 1994 the state legislature set a ceiling on the programme of 1.5 per cent of Milwaukee's 100,000 school-aged population, or 1,500 students. The private schools participating in the programme must limit voucher students to 49 per cent of their student body, which limits the number of places available. Since the programme's inception, the lack of space has meant that more students have been turned away than have been accepted into the programme. In consequence, spaces are apportioned by lottery (McGroaty, 1994).

The Milwaukee scheme, though small, warrants attention because it is the only source of hard evidence on the effects of vouchers in the United States. Comments on the programme's performance have been based on the annual reports of Professor John F. Witte, the state-selected outside evaluator. His first reports led some critics to complain that the participating schools suffered excessive attrition (drop-outs) and that achievement tests were biased because the mothers of the families using vouchers had a higher average high-school completion rate than mothers of students who did not use vouchers. These complaints were later rebutted by McGroaty (1994).

Those findings among Witte's evaluations that are unambiguously positive, meanwhile, combat three of the popular fears or predictions about the voucher programme, discussed in greater detail in the next section. The first is the suspicion that vouchers will help individuals who are not poor and who therefore need help least. Witte's evidence shows, on the contrary, that 'choice families' are among the poorest of the poor. Their average income in 1994 was $11,625 – half the income level of the average family with children in Milwaukee's public schools.

The second commonly expressed fear is that vouchers will lead to segregated and anti-social schools. Evidence supplied by Witte shows instead that the Milwaukee programme fosters diversity and that no participating school has been teaching cultural supremacy or separation: 'The student bodies of participating [voucher] schools vary from schools that are almost all one minority race, to racially integrated schools, to schools that have used the Choice program to diversify their almost all-white student bodies' (Witte et al., 1995: 15).

The third fear – that voucher schools will skim off the 'cream' of the student 'crop' – is countered by Witte's finding that 'the program is offering opportunities for a private school alternative to poor families whose children were not succeeding in school. This is a positive outcome of the program' (p. 16).

Other positive conclusions from Witte's reports include the finding of high parental involvement, once in the system, and high parental satisfaction with the programme – in particular, that it increased learning and discipline. 'Respondents almost unanimously agreed the program should continue' (p. 17).

The case for vouchers rests also on the argued need to weaken the public school monopoly or, in other words, to promote competition. But when competition is introduced, those suppliers who initially lose, or expect to lose, customers will, in self-defence, act to raise the quality of their services. Applied to our education context, five years of the Milwaukee plan is more than enough time for the threatened public schools to have improved under the pressure of new voucher competition. And in so far as vouchers can take some credit for inducing the improvements in tested achievement that have in fact occurred over the years 1990–96 (in public and private schools), findings of no current difference in achievement growth between public and voucher (choice) schools do not unambiguously imply that vouchers have failed to improve efficiency.

The future of vouchers in the United States will obviously be influenced not only by official annual reports, but also by the assessments and responses of the parents. The fact that demand for voucher places in Milwaukee currently well exceeds supply could already be pressuring politicians to allow more families to participate.

United Kingdom

(Editors' note: each of the schemes described by E. G. West here was abolished by the incoming Labour government in 1997.)

In 1981 the Assisted Places Scheme was established in the United Kingdom with the aim of providing a ladder of opportunity for able but poor students. Under the scheme today, low-income parents can obtain assistance with tuition fees for an independent school if the school has been approved by the Department of Education and Science.

By 1995 about 29,800 students were using these selective vouchers at 294 specified independent schools in England (there is a separate system for Scotland). About 5,000 new pupils enter the programme every year, mostly at the ages of eleven or thirteen.

The English experience raises two questions that have implications for the general debate on vouchers discussed in the next section. First, why – in view of the government's stated wish to encourage competition and 'market discipline' – is the Assisted Places method so limited in coverage (see UK Department of Education, 1992)? Second, why are the places limited mainly to able pupils who exhibit the potential for high academic achievement, when such pupils can expect a higher-than-average lifetime income whether or not they are in Assisted Places? The contrast with Milwaukee's selective voucher scheme, where the low-income students designated for help have not been succeeding in school, is striking.

The voucher principle has also been extended in the United Kingdom to further education and (prospectively) to nursery schooling. Further education colleges (similar to community colleges in the United States) have recently been re-established as autonomous institutions independent of their former local governments. A new system of 'learning agreements' – effectively, individual contracts between a college and a student, specifying the precise qualifications aimed for – enables government funding to follow the student to the college of his or her choice. At the pre-school level, the Department of Education declared in 1995 that it was about to extend free entitlement for all four-year-olds to good-quality private, as well as public, nursery education (World Bank, 1995: 4.1). Currently the initiative has been limited to two pilot schemes in East Anglia. The plan, however, is to be extended to all four-year-olds in April 1997 (*The Economist*, 1996).

The current debate on vouchers

As the case for parental choice and competition has gained in popularity, the criticism of those antipathetic to vouchers has increased in intensity. Debate has focused on the potential effects of vouchers on the public benefits connected with education; the possibilities for damage to the quality of public schools on the one hand or to the identity and autonomy of private schools on the other; their impact, if any, on poverty; the issue of windfall gains for the middle class; and the possible effect of a voucher system on the government's administrative costs.

Vouchers and the marketplace

Some view vouchers primarily in terms of a free market which vouchers would encourage. They then see this as a prime example of 'economic man' sacrificing social welfare to his selfish pursuit of individual material gain. But economists have long since abandoned narrow assumptions about self-interest. As Becker (1993: 385–6) observes: 'Behavior is driven by a much richer set of values and preferences. [My] analysis assumes that individuals maximize welfare as *they conceive it*, whether they be selfish, altruistic, loyal, spiteful, or masochistic.' A pertinent example is the objections made by the members of the Polish Civic Educational Association in the late 1980s to the national school system inherited from the collapsed communist regime. Their position was that they wanted to maximise welfare as *they* as individuals saw it, as a welcome change from having welfare defined and imposed by totalitarian authorities or highly centralised bureaucracies. The type of institutions they demanded were non-state (including religious) private or independent schools (Glenn, 1995: 127).

A related argument by opponents of vouchers is that a free market would lead to discrimination on grounds of race or disability. Krashinsky (1986: 143) argues that vouchers could lead to racial segregation. The usual reply here is to quote Coleman's (1990) findings that segregation is in fact greater in public than in private schools. Shanker and Rosenberg (1992) suggest in the same vein as Krashinsky that profit-making schools would reject difficult-to-educate children under a voucher system. Lieberman

(1991a) found, on the contrary, that the single largest US group of for-profit schools serves the disabled. Blum (1985), meanwhile, provides evidence that urban private schools maintain a higher level of discipline than do public schools.

Another common argument against vouchers is that parents cannot be expected to make sound choices for their children (Bridge, 1978; Carnegie Foundation, 1992; Levin, 1991; Wells and Crain, 1992). Others reply that parents simply need some initial experience (hitherto denied them) at making such choices in order to become more adept. A second response is that, in a democracy, any serious impediments to decision-making by parents will show up also at the ballot box when they choose political representatives to make decisions on education. A third response is to quote empirical studies demonstrating rational choice for their children by parents who themselves have only modest amounts of education (Fossey, 1994).

A further concern – that vouchers (or tax credits) for education might introduce fraudulent practices – is put forward by Murnane (1983), who draws an analogy with food stamps in the United States. Experience there, he observes, shows that unscrupulous parties make claims for fictitious individuals. Schmidt (1995) shows that serious shortcomings of fraud and dishonesty are already present in the public school system. Moreover, and to reiterate, the school voucher largely avoids the black market problem because it is difficult to transfer the rights to education.

Public versus private benefits from education

It is generally accepted that a child's education provides not only private benefits to the family (mainly by prospectively increasing income), but also public benefits (positive externalities). The latter include poverty reduction, economic growth, and the pursuit of common values (see Krashinsky, 1986). The economic model supporting this argument is that of 'joint supply'. One classical example of it is wool production: wool cannot be produced without simultaneously producing meat, and vice versa. Furthermore, a switch from one breed of sheep to another is likely to improve the wool production at the expense of meat, or the converse. Similarly, so the argument goes, the cost of more or improved public benefits from education shows up in fewer, or worse-quality, private benefits, introducing an interesting trade-off problem. The public benefits are quite distinct from the private. Thus the inducement to an orderly society that educated citizens bring is one example of a public benefit. The increase in expected lifetime income that education bestows on students is, in contrast, an example of a purely private benefit.

Some economists object to free choice of schooling through a voucher system because they believe families will not trade off private for public benefits but will allocate their expenditures on the basis of their private benefits exclusively. In other words, the valuation that others in society place upon the education of one's child will be neglected, and public benefits will suffer relative to private benefits – the well-known 'public good problem'.

Proponents of that view, such as Krashinsky (1986) and Levin (1991), claim that public schools have a unique ability to produce the 'common values' just mentioned. But this claim also is now contested. Cohn (1979), for instance, observes that, in practice, public schools in the United States have successfully resisted attempts to homogenise their procedures, so that 'a student in one school district might receive an entirely different set of common values than his counterpart in another school district' (p. 262). Nevertheless, the belief that public schools possess an absolute advantage in producing the 'public good' benefits remains strongly entrenched among educationists as well as among some economists.

Private schools are direct producers of externalities (Hettich, 1969), and they also generate them *indirectly* (West, 1991). It is generally agreed that private schools are more efficient at producing private benefits, through more effective teaching of the basics, such as literacy. This is so partly because public schools are monopolies, while private schools have greater output per dollar because they experience competition. But literacy is also a public benefit, a necessary condition for communicating common values and fostering economic growth. This indirect assistance by private schooling to the production of such public benefits is at least as important as the direct production.

Krashinsky (1986) focuses on what he calls transaction costs, such as the costs of communication in obtaining the public benefits of education. His position is that these costs are too high for the government to contract out to private suppliers because the public benefits 'are so subtle' (p. 155). Even if this were the case, family consumers of private benefits from education could equally claim, bearing in mind the variety of cultural aspirations, that the education quality they seek is so inarticulable that the transaction costs of delegating the task to governments are prohibitive. In any case a central government still faces similar transaction costs in issuing instructions to thousands of school districts, which in turn face even higher costs in supervising tens of thousands of individual public schools.

The public good argument, as employed by Krashinsky, contains a serious theoretical flaw. The classical example of a public good is that of the fishermen who need a lighthouse. Even though all the fishermen in a given area would benefit from the beam of light generated, each one will conceal his true preferences and wait for others to provide it. But because each fisherman in turn will behave in the same way and try to 'free-ride', the lighthouse will not be built. Because there is no mechanism parallel to the usual market system leading to the revelation of sincere (true) preferences, so it is argued, we have a case of 'market failure'. In the context of education the preferences that are not revealed are those of the 'neighbours' who value the education for separate reasons. Krashinsky's assumption is that the problem will be solved by government intervention. But he assumes unjustifiably that the government possesses all knowledge of the relevant preferences of each and every neighbour. And even if government were to consult everyone individually, individual neighbours would have no more incentive to reveal their true preferences to government than they would in the conventional market. Government failure therefore matches the market failure.

Potential damage to the public school system

Unions of public school teachers and administrators frequently contend that a voucher system will destroy the public school system. Krashinsky (1986), for example, argues that middle- and upper-class parents would desert the public system in favour of private schools that discriminate in various ways against poor, disadvantaged or minority applicants. The poor would be left in gutted, underfunded and decaying public schools. But this argument rests on the questionable assumption that the public system will refuse to adjust in the face of competition from private schools

(Wilkinson, 1994). Holmes (1988: 23) maintains that 'there is no reason why inner city schools of the future, where alternatives are available [with vouchers], will be worse than the ones at the moment where there is no choice'. In addition, Krashinsky's fear that middle-income parents will desert the public school system with the aid of vouchers has no basis where they are allotted exclusively to low-income families, as they are today in such widely different countries as Bangladesh, Chile, Colombia, Puerto Rico, the United Kingdom and the United States. By most reports, such systems are improving the condition of the poor relative to those in the rest of society.

Vouchers and poverty reduction

Krashinsky's implicit assumption is that the public school system benefits the poor in a way that is superior to any alternative. But low-income families are segregated residentially, and their children are typically allocated to the schools nearest their homes. If they want to choose a better public school in a middle-class area, they must purchase a home there, and the housing prices are usually beyond their means. Middle-class families, by contrast, can move more easily because they are less restricted financially. The result is that the public provision of schooling becomes heterogeneous, with the poor, on average, receiving the worst quality. Vouchers would help remove the barriers to mobility.

Friedman and Friedman (1980) insist that they too favour reducing poverty and promoting equal opportunity, but argue that in both respects the voucher system would unmistakably improve things. They contend that liberty, equality of opportunity and the reduction of poverty are complementary and not competitive goals of the voucher system. Their main argument is that lower-income families, trapped in large city ghetto schools, would benefit most from vouchers. 'Are the supermarkets available to different economic groups anything like so divergent in quality as the schools?' they ask. 'Vouchers would improve the quality of the public schooling available to the rich hardly at all; to the middle class, moderately; to the low-income class, enormously' (p. 169).

Windfall gains for the middle class

Some opponents of vouchers focus on what they call the inequitable windfall gains for families (usually well-to-do) that customarily purchase private education. In other words costs to governments would increase if vouchers (or tax credits) were extended to rich private school clients not now financed by government (Gemello and Osman, 1983). Seldon (1986) points out, however, that total costs to government could fall depending on the value of the voucher as a proportion of per capita public school costs. The government savings would occur, according to Friedman (in Seldon 1986: 20), if the voucher value was 75 per cent of public school costs. The reasoning is that the economies effected by migrants from public to private schools, who would now cost the government 25 per cent less than before, would offset the cost of the windfall gain to accustomed users of private schools. (Clearly, because a strong argument put forward by voucher supporters is that private schools can deliver at lower costs than public, their case looks more consistent if they demand vouchers at values less than 100 per cent of average per pupil costs in public schools.)

The windfall gains problem could also be handled by making vouchers subject to tax. But selective voucher systems, restricted to low-income families, would be even more effective – indeed, such selective vouchers would automatically prevent high-income families now patronising private schools from enjoying the windfall gains.

Regulatory threats to private school identity

A potential drawback to vouchers has recently been suggested by strong believers in the philosophy of freedom, who want to see more competition in schooling but fear that voucher systems would seriously threaten the autonomy of independent schools. Currently the most articulate and influential spokesman for this point of view in the United States is Sheldon Richman (1994). In his words: 'It is likely that before schools could accept vouchers, they would be required to meet a raft of standards that before long would make the private schools virtually indistinguishable from public schools' (p. 83). Voucher initiatives that insisted on zero regulation would stand no chance of acceptance, Richman says, because, 'as the opposition would inevitably point out, the voucher plan would appear to authorize appropriation of "public" money to institutions not accountable to "public authorities"' (p. 84). In the same vein, Gary North (1993) argues: 'We will have federal guidelines operating in every voucher using school, equal opportunity policies and quota systems of every kind, teaching hiring and firing policies, racially and religiously mixed student bodies. There will be a whole army of federal bureaucrats, not to mention state bureaucrats policing every "private" school' (p. 149).

Friedman has always separated three levels of issues: first, whether schooling should be compulsory; second, whether it should be financed privately or by the government; and third, how it should be organised. His position has been that whatever one's views may be on the first two issues, a voucher scheme would produce a better and more effective organisation than the present one – that is, vouchers remain a superior alternative to a system of schools run and financed by government. Like North and Richman, Friedman sees benefits also in eventually removing compulsion and government finance, but he is primarily concerned with the question of how to get there from here. Vouchers, he believes, are still a practical transitional measure (Friedman, 1993).

As for the threat of a government regulatory takeover of private schools, Henderson (1993) points out that these institutions do not have to accept vouchers with all their strings. Others argue also that the recipients of vouchers can and will lobby their government against heavy regulation. Lieberman (1991a: 6), meanwhile, argues that the more likely cause of increased regulation will be the political objections to funding both public and private schools while closely regulating only the former. Consequently, Lieberman observes, supporters of vouchers must argue that to approach parity what is needed is reduction of the regulation of public schools, not an increase in the regulation of private schools.

The costs of implementation

A common concern about the administrative costs of implementing a voucher system is whether the size of the bureaucracy necessary to oversee the total system will have to expand significantly. Wilkinson (1994) finds no reason to believe that costs such as those associated with monitoring student attendance and quality of education should be any higher for private than for public schools; school quality can be overseen by periodic inspections in the same way as it is in public schools. Even in the unlikely event that administrative costs did rise, such an increase would be more than offset by the savings realised given the evidence cited above that private schooling generally costs less than public. Tax-funded vouchers in the countries described in Table 4 are typically valued at considerably less than the public school per capita cost; the Milwaukee plan, for instance, supplies students with vouchers worth about half of the public school cost. It is highly improbable that additional administrative costs could equal such a huge differential. Indeed, a strong argument for governments to use vouchers is the need in these days of budgetary stringency to economise on public spending.

Final comments

The main purpose of this chapter has been to provide information on the theory and practice of education vouchers throughout the world and to summarise briefly the principal points raised in current academic and political debates on the issue. Absence of real-world evidence has until recently hampered discussion – indeed, until recently has been adduced by several writers to demonstrate that vouchers were not desirable. But emerging evidence (see Table 4) suggests otherwise, and this may well be due to changing circumstances.

During the last two decades governments have become increasingly unwilling or unable to continue to raise the share of public expenditure spent on education. The prime focus has switched accordingly to attempts to obtain higher output from given expenditure levels. The use of vouchers valued at much less than 100 per cent of the cost per pupil in public schools has already been successful in Sweden, Milwaukee (United States) and

Poland, and may become a popular way of economising. Economists, meanwhile, see the key role in such efficiency gains to be the gradual removal of the current monopoly structure in education.

It is too early to reach firm general conclusions about the effectiveness of vouchers. There are only twenty entries in the table, and these show a wide variety of design. Those who fear that government regulations associated with vouchers will ultimately strangle the individuality of private schools will insist that this may yet happen. Nonetheless, significant numbers of families are now obtaining positive first-hand experience with private schooling through voucher systems. This phenomenon alone could well alter the political climate in their favour.

References

(The term 'processed' describes informally reproduced works that may not be commonly available through library systems.)

Becker, Gary S. (1993), 'The Economic Way of Looking at Behavior', Nobel Lecture, *Journal of Political Economy* 101(3): 385–409.

Becker, Gary S. (1995), 'Human Capital and Poverty Alleviation', HRO Working Paper no. 52, World Bank, Washington, DC. Processed.

Blum, V. C. (1985), 'Private Elementary Education in the Inner City', *Phi Delta Kappan* 66(9): 645–8.

Bridge, Gary (1978), 'Information Imperfections. The Achilles Heel of Entitlement Plans', *School Review* 86(37): 504–29.

Carnegie Foundation for the Advancement of Teaching (1992), *School Choice*, Princeton, NJ.

Cohn, Elchanan (1979), *The Economics of Education*, Ballinger, Cambridge, MA.

Coleman, James (1990), *Equality and Achievement in Education*, Westview Press, Boulder, CO.

Easton, Stephen T. (1988), *Education in Canada*, Fraser Institute, Vancouver, Canada.

Economist, The (1996), 'Catch 'em Young', 26 October, p. 68.

'Education Vouchers in Practice & Principle: A World Survey' (full report). Available on request from the author at Carleton University, Department of Economics, 1125 Colonel By Drive, Ottawa K1S 5116, Canada. Processed.

Flew, Antony (1995), *All the Right Places*, Adam Smith Institute, London.

Fossey, Robert (1994), 'Open Enrollment in Massachusetts: Why Families Choose', *Education Evaluation and Policy Analysis* 16(3): 320–34.

Friedman, Milton (1993), 'Letter to the Editor', *Freeman*, July, p. 321.

Friedman, Milton and Rose (1980), *Free to Choose: A Personal Statement*, Harcourt Brace Jovanovich, New York.

Gemello, John, and Jack Osman (1983), 'The Choice for Public and Private Education: An Economist's View', in Thomas James and Henry M. Levin (eds), *Public Dollars for Private Schools*, Temple University Press, Philadelphia, PA.

Glenn, Charles L. (1995), *Educational Freedom in Eastern Europe*, CATO Institute, Washington, DC.

Henderson, David R. (1993), 'Why We Need School Choice', *Insight* 43(10): 26–9.

Hettich, Walter (1969), 'Mixed Public and Private Financing of Education: Comment', *American Economic Review* 59: 210–12.

Holmes, Mark (1988), 'The Funding of Independent Schools', in James E. Lam and G. Benjamin (eds), *Public Policy and Private Education in Japan*, Macmillan, London.

Krashinsky, Michael (1986), 'Why Educational Vouchers May Be Bad Economics', *Teachers College Record* 88(2): 139–51.

Levin, Henry M. (1991), 'The Economics of Educational Choice', *Economics of Education Review* 10(2): 137–58.

Lieberman, Myron (1991a), 'The Case for Voluntary Funding of Education', Policy Study 37, Heartland Institute, Chicago, IL. Processed.

Lieberman, Myron (1991b), *Privatization and Education Choice*. St Martin's Press, New York.

Lockheed, Marlaine E., and Emmanuel Jimenez (1994), 'Public and Private Secondary Schools in Developing Countries', HRO Working Paper no. 43, World Bank, Washington, DC. Processed.

Lynn, Robert (1986), 'The Japanese Example of Indirect Vouchers', *Economic Affairs* 6(6): 25–7.

Matte, Patricia, and Antonio Sancho (1993), 'Primary and Secondary Education', in Christian Larroulet (ed.), *Private Solutions to Public Problems*, Instituto Libertad y Desarrolo, Santiago, Chile.

McGroaty, Daniel (1994), 'School Choice Slandered', *The Public Interest* 117: 32–41.

Murnane, Richard J. (1983), 'The Uncertain Consequences of Tuition Tax Credits: An Analysis of Student Achievement and Economic Incentives', in Thomas James and Henry M. Levin (eds), *Public Dollars for Private Schools*, Temple University Press, Philadelphia, PA.

National Program of Self-Administration for Educational Development (PRONADE), October 1996.

North, Gary (1993), 'Education Vouchers: The Double Tax', *Freeman* 43(6): 72–81.

Oakland, William (1994), 'Fiscal Equity', in John E. Anderson
    (ed.), *Fiscal Equalization for State and Local Government
    Finance*, Praeger, London.

OECD (Organisation for Economic Cooperation and
    Development) (1994), *School: A Matter of Choice*, Paris.

Richman, Sheldon (1994), *Separating School and State*, Future of
    Freedom Foundation, Fairfax, VA.

Schmidt, Paul (1995), 'Looking the Other Way', *Education Week*
    14(21): 23–7.

Seldon, Arthur (1986), *The Riddle of the Voucher*, Hobart
    Paperback 21, Institute of Economic Affairs, London.

Shanker, Albert, and Brian Rosenberg (1992, 'Politics, Markets,
    and American Schools: A Rejoinder', in P. R. Kane (ed.),
    Independent Schools, Independent Thinkers, Jossey-Bass, San
    Francisco, CA.

Tucker, Allyson M., and William F. Lauber (eds) (1995), *School
    Choice Programs: What's Happening in the States*, Heritage
    Foundation, Washington, DC.

UK Department of Education (1992), *Choice and Diversity*, London.

Walberg, Herbert J., and Joseph L. Bast (1993), 'School Choice:
    The Essential Reform', CATO *Journal* 13(1).

Wells, A. S., and R. L. Crain (1992), 'Do Parents Choose School
    Quality or School Status? A Sociological Theory of Free
    Market Education', in P. W. Cookson (ed.), *The Choice
    Controversy*, Corwin Press, Newbury Park, NY.

West, Edwin G. (1991), 'Public Schools and Excess Burdens',
    Economics of Education Review 10(2).

Wilkinson, Bruce (1994), 'Educational Choice: Necessary but Not
    Sufficient', Institute for Research on Public Policy, Montreal,
    Canada.

Winkler, Donald R., and Taryn Rounds (1993), 'Municipal and Private Sector Response to Decentralization and School Choice', HRO Working Paper 8, World Bank, Washington, DC. Processed.

Witte, John F. et al. (1995), 'Fourth Year Report', Milwaukee Parental Choice Program, Department of Public Instruction, Madison, WI.

World Bank (1995), 'Education Reform in the United Kingdom: Autonomy with Accountability', Human Development Department, Washington, DC. Processed.

10 EDUCATION WITHOUT THE STATE
E. G. West[1]

To conjecture a Britain that had never experienced government intervention in education is not without problems. It would be helpful, for instance, if we could point to the experience of another country similar in all respects but without 'free' and compulsory state education. Yet this is hardly possible because government intervention prevails throughout Western countries and seems to be the inevitable consequence of the growth of political democracy.

The historical attachment to democracy is sometimes explained as the need to protect the poor. But since democracy is a simple majority voting institution, how can we expect the poor, who constitute a minority, to be particularly well served?

Pressure groups, politicians, bureaucrat self-interest

More sophisticated observers in the economic school of public choice are now viewing democracy as an institution operated largely by special interest groups, vote-maximising politicians and self-seeking bureaucracies, which do not represent the poor. Many scholars now conclude that the eventual dominant objective of government school systems is not to promote the greatest

---

1   This essay originally appeared in *Economic Affairs*, October 1994.

happiness of parents or children, or the most efficient schooling, but to transfer wealth to educators. In line with this view, education illustrates, indeed, one of the most glaring examples of rent-seeking – the extraction of privileges from government – that the world has ever seen.

If the government school system is so firmly attached to politics, is it not merely academic to imagine Britain without its state education while continuing with its democracy? There are at least three possible responses.

1. *First*, because democracy can appear in several varieties, it would be enlightening to conjecture the differences in education that could result from variations in constitutional rules and structures. They would include more inclusive voting rules (reinforced as distinct from simple majority voting), decentralisation as opposed to central government dominance, restrictions and/or extensions of the franchise, and increased use of referenda.

2. *Second*, even if it now seems impossible to return to a world of almost negligible state involvement in education, it is still a useful undertaking to correct public misunderstanding about schooling before the famous Forster Act of 1870, which introduced government schools.

3. *Third*, since the present extent of rent-seeking depends on differences in the volume of information about education possessed (a) by the suppliers (teachers and officials) and (b) by the voters at large, the equilibrium could eventually change, at least at the margin, as parents, families and members of the general public

became more informed. This essay will focus on the second and the third of these possibilities.

An extension of the pre-1870 trends without the 1870 act

Henry Brougham's Select Committee reported (in 1820) that in 1818 about one in seventeen of the total population of England & Wales was being schooled, paid for largely by working parents. If education is a 'normal' economic good, we would expect this measure of schooling to increase with the rise in incomes. Brougham's committee reported that the figures for 1818 were a considerable improvement in eighteen years on 1800 when the earliest estimate was made. Ten years later, in 1828, Brougham, in his private capacity, followed up the report for 1818 with a 5 per cent sample survey of his own, using the same sources (the parochial clergy) as before. His findings suggested that the number of children in schools had doubled.

Such evidence alone would challenge the view that the desire for education has to be *imposed by* the state. If education 'consumption' begins to appear and to rise with income, the most appropriate government strategy might be one or more of the following:

- redistribution of income to enable more parents to pay;
- more patience at a time of steady income growth; and
- concentration on removal of barriers to such growth.

The rising income correlation with the growth in education suggests that, as income per head increased in the nineteenth century, schooling grew 'vigorously' in response. Whereas the actual growth of income per head in the years 1801–71 was slightly over 1 per cent per annum, the average annual growth rate of day scholars was well over 2 per cent. The growth of schooling in England & Wales during this period, it should be emphasised, came before it was made free, compulsory and supplied by government. The major nineteenth-century legislation came in 1870 with the Forster Act. Yet by 1869 *most* people in England & Wales were literate, *most* children were receiving a schooling and *most* parents, working class included, were paying fees for it.[2] It is surely reasonable to suggest that since per capita income continued to grow after 1858, both the number of day scholars and the average years of school attendance would have continued to grow. Since, moreover, there would have been no crowding out of private by government schools, the private sector would have continued to be diverse, with denominational church schools playing a much stronger role than after the Forster Act.

The savings in the costs of taxation

After 1870 the direct spending on education by individual families was replaced by indirect spending for them via government. To accomplish this feat government had to increase taxation. By the 1990s the sources of taxation for state schooling have become numerous and the total revenue required has vastly expanded. At this point we have to focus on one of the major economic consequences of the collectivisation of schooling, well understood by economists but usually neglected by

2   Edwin G. West, *Education and the State*, Institute of Economic Affairs, London, 1965; 2nd edn, 1970, p. xvii; 3rd edn (revised and extended), Liberty Fund, Indianapolis, IN, 1994.

educationists and laymen partly because it seems excessively theoretical. The economic concept of the deadweight welfare cost of taxation stems from the fact that instead of a 'perfect' tax system that uses lump-sum taxes for all revenue purposes, we impose a variety of taxes each of which causes distortions in consumption and/or resource allocation. Income taxes, for instance, cause distortions in the choices between leisure and work, excise taxes cause 'artificial' contractions of consumption of the taxed goods, and so on.

An example outlines the main issues. Suppose an excise tax is levied on television receivers, thus causing an increase in price, but so high that the output falls to zero. No tax revenue is collected, and there is no direct cost of taxation (no withdrawal of private sector resources). But clearly there is another burden. Too few television sets are produced and too many other commodities. There is a misallocation of resources. We know that, without the tax, consumers had a preference for a certain quantity of television receivers and a smaller quantity of other goods. After the tax they are constrained to distort their purchases into a less preferred pattern. Consumers are obviously worse off with the resource allocation caused by the tax. This burden, or 'deadweight welfare cost', exists even though there is no direct cost of revenue collection from the tax. This example shows that, although the two types of burdens are descriptively different, they are both costs in the economist's sense. In the more typical situation, an excise tax is not so high as to reduce production to zero (and some tax revenue is raised). In this case, the two burdens of tax, the direct cost and the deadweight welfare cost, coexist.

It is important to realise that the deadweight cost of taxation increases exponentially with increases in the share of the GNP taken by government.[3] Since this share is larger in Britain than in the USA, the calculations of deadweight cost magnitudes are even higher for Britain. Usher[4] demonstrates that the conventional deadweight loss analysis adopted by US writers[5] underestimates the cost of raising government revenue because it ignores the welfare cost of tax evasion. This cost also increases exponentially with the share of GNP taken by government. Incorporating tax evasion costs, Usher calculates that, with a government share of GNP of 50 per cent and tax evasion of 10 per cent, it costs 80 pence to raise £1 of extra tax revenue. In other words, the total burden on taxpayers when one extra pound of revenue is raised amounts to £1.80.

Judging from the recent economic literature as a whole, it seems reasonable to conclude that the deadweight costs of the taxes used to supply revenues for British state education in the 1990s amount to at least 50 per cent of the direct costs of that education. Assuming there had been no Forster Act, therefore, citizens in the late nineteenth century would have been spared these excessive costs. But the main significance of this examination of the tax cost applies to the present time, when the share of British government in GNP is around an all-time high and the deadweight costs have increased dramatically. Thus if, starting with the year 1870, government had not intervened in the expansion of schooling, it is probable today (in 1994) that we would be

---

3   E. K and J. M. Browning, *Public Finance and the Price System*, Macmillan, New York, 3rd edn, 1987, for instance, assume that the cost grows by roughly the square of the increase in the size of the government's share of GNP.

4   Dan Usher, 'Tax Evasion and the Marginal Cost of Public Funds', *Economic Inquiry* XXIV(4), 1986, pp. 563–86.

5   For example, C. L. Ballard, J. A. Shoven and J. Whalley, 'General Equilibrium Computations on the Marginal Welfare Costs of Taxation', *American Economic Review* 75(1), 1985.

spared the unprecedented excess costs in taxation for financing state education.

In British private education before 1870, the record of educational outputs such as literacy was even more impressive than the numbers of children in school, and presents an even more serious problem to typical authors of social histories. Professor Mark Blaug has observed that 'Conventional histories of education neatly dispose of the problem by simply ignoring the literacy evidence.'[6] He emphasises that, since it is common in developing countries for literacy to run ahead of the numbers in school, we have to recognise the existence of numerous educational agencies outside formal state schooling.

These agencies in the nineteenth century included the adult education movement, the mutual improvement societies, the literary and philosophical institutes, the mechanics' institutes and the Owenite halls of science. Professor Blaug also refers to freelance lecturers who travelled the towns and stimulated self-study among the poor. And in part-time formal education the Sunday schools and adult evening schools were obvious examples. Simultaneously also, there were the factory schools 'which proliferated in the northern textile industry long before the 1833 Act made them mandatory'.[7]

From this impressive collection of agencies outside the formal state education system, paid by parents, grandparents, employers, charities and other private sources, it is clear that they would have continued and probably strengthened had there been no Forster Act in 1870.

---

6   Mark Blaug, 'The Economics of Education in English Classical Political Economy: A Re-examination', in A. Skinner and T. Wilson, *Essays on Adam Smith*, Clarendon Press, Oxford, 1975, p. 595.

7   Ibid., p. 597.

Non-profit institutions

The government schools that were introduced after 1870 were non-profit institutions and they came eventually to enjoy strong monopoly powers. One of the serious weaknesses of non-profit organisations is their sluggish response to dynamic change. Suppose, for instance, new cost-saving (or output-increasing) methods become available that have not been widely adopted so far. In a for-profit free market system, entrepreneurs would incorporate the new methods and would seize the corresponding opportunities for entry stimulated by direct and clear income-gaining incentives. In a world of non-profit organisations, in contrast, such incentives do not exist. There are no conventional entrepreneurs, only administrators. Prompt and widespread entry by innovators is therefore not to be expected.

But does the problem apply also to the private schools, many, if not most, of which are also non-profit institutions? The efficiency obstacles here are not so serious. Managers of a non-profit private school are normally sensitive to the vital contribution of donations to their budget (and therefore their personal incomes), as a direct function of the school's reputation. In addition, private school fees make a decisive difference. When a parent withdraws a child the fee income automatically decreases and places immediate pressure on management. Government school headmasters, in contrast, have no such direct economic pressure from their parent-customers.

Even though most of the private schools might have remained non-profit organisations after 1870 without the Forster Act, they would have been subject to increasing competition from the vast array of the non-formal private education agencies. This competition would have been strengthened in the absence of compulsion, for there would have continued to be a legal right to quit formal education and to seek the competing informal private alternatives at any time. The effect of compulsion has usually been to strengthen the monopoly power of the government school, especially when, as happened in the late nineteenth century, the average family's income was pre-empted through indirect (regressive) taxes on goods and services to finance the so-called 'free' schooling available only in state schools.

Conclusion

The fluid, flexible, heterogeneous and competitive educational scenario of the pre-1870s is the environment that the more radical of reformers of education are now demanding in many countries. The choice of school movement, it is maintained, has been to a large extent misinformed. What is needed is choice in *education*. School choice has not and will not lead to more productive education because the obsolete technology called 'school' is inherently *inelastic*. As long as 'school' refers to the traditional structure of buildings and grounds with services delivered in boxes called classrooms to which customers must be transported by car or bus, 'school choice' will be unable to meaningfully alter the quality or efficiency of education.[8]

Although this argument is perhaps extreme it contains a substantial truth. Genuinely free markets are unpredictable in their unfolding school organisations as well as in their offerings of completely new curricula with which they constantly surprise us. The post-1870 era without the Forster Act provided precisely

---

8   Lewis Perleman, *School's Out*, Avon Books, New York, 1992, pp. 186–7.

the setting necessary for the emergence of a truly dynamic and innovative *education* market in the 1990s. It is unfortunate that this market was destroyed by the combined action of politicians, bureaucrats and rent-seekers, action that not only reduced the potential quality of education but also imposed on citizens enormous financial burdens, especially in the deadweight costs of taxation.

EPILOGUE: YES PRIME MINISTER –
THE NATIONAL EDUCATION SERVICE
Antony Jay & Jonathan Lynn[1]

I called Humphrey in first thing this morning. Dorothy was with me. I tried to disguise my excitement as I casually told him that I wanted to bounce a new idea off him.

The word 'new' usually alerts Humphrey that trouble's in store, but this time he seemed perfectly relaxed and actually chuckled when I told him that I've realised how to reform our education system.

So I let him have it. 'Humphrey, I'm going to let parents take their children away from schools. They will be able to move them to any school they want.'

He was unconcerned. 'You mean, after application, scrutiny, tribunal hearing and appeal procedures?'

It was my turn to chuckle. 'No, Humphrey. They could just move them. Whenever they want.'

'I'm sorry, Prime Minister, I don't follow you.' I could see that he genuinely didn't understand.

Dorothy spelled it out, abrasively. 'The government, Sir Humphrey, is going to let parents decide which school to send their children to.'

Suddenly he understood that we actually meant what we were

---

1   Originally appeared as *Yes Prime Minister*, 'The National Education Service', series 2, no. 7, 1988, reprinted by kind permission of Antony Jay and Jonathan Lynn.

saying. He exploded into protest. 'Prime Minister, you're not serious?'

I nodded benevolently. 'Yes I am.'

'But that's preposterous!'

'Why?' asked Dorothy.

He ignored her completely. 'You can't let parents make these choices. How on earth would parents know which schools are best?'

Coolly I appraised him. 'What school did you go to, Humphrey?'

'Winchester.'

'Was it good?' I asked politely.

'Excellent, of course.'

'Who chose it?'

'My parents, naturally.' I smiled at him. 'Prime Minister, that's quite different. My parents were discerning people. You can't expect *ordinary* people to know where to send their children.'

Dorothy was manifestly shocked at Humphrey's snobbery and elitism. 'Why on earth not?'

He shrugged. The answer was obvious to him. 'How could they tell?'

Dorothy, a mother herself, found the question only too easy to answer. 'They could tell if their kids could read and write and do sums. They could tell if the neighbours were happy with the school. They could tell if the exam results aren't good.'

Again he studiously ignored her. 'Examinations aren't everything, Prime Minister.'

Dorothy stood up, moved around the cabinet table and sat down very close to me so that Humphrey could no longer avoid meeting her eyes. 'That is true, Humphrey – and those parents who don't want an academic education for their kids could choose progressive schools.'

I could see that, as far as Humphrey was concerned, Dorothy and I were talking ancient Chinese. He simply didn't understand us. Again he tried to explain his position, and he was becoming quite emotional. 'Parents are not qualified to make these choices. Teachers are the professionals. In fact, parents are the worst people to bring up children, they have no qualifications for it. We don't allow untrained teachers to teach. The same would apply to parents in an ideal world.'

I realised with stunning clarity, and for the very first time, how far Humphrey's dream of an ideal world differed from mine. 'You mean,' I asked slowly and quietly, 'parents should be stopped from having kids until they've been trained?'

He sighed impatiently. Apparently I'd missed the point. 'No, no. Having kids isn't the problem. They've all been trained to *have* kids, sex education classes have been standard for years now.'

'I see,' I said, and turned to Dorothy, who was wide-eyed in patent disbelief at our most senior civil servant and advocate of the Orwellian corporate state. 'Perhaps,' I suggested, 'we can improve on the sex education classes? Before people have children we could give them exams. Written and practical. Or both, perhaps? Then we could issue breeding licences.'

Humphrey wasn't a bit amused. He ticked me off. 'There's no need to be facetious, Prime Minister. I'm being serious. It's *looking after* children that parents are not qualified for. That's why they have no idea how to choose schools for them. It couldn't work.'

Dorothy leaned across in front of me, to catch his eye. 'Then how does the Health Service work? People choose their family doctor without having medical qualifications.'

'Ah,' said Humphrey, playing for time. 'Yes,' he said, flummoxed. 'That's different,' he concluded, as if he'd actually said something.

'Why?' asked Dorothy.

'Well, doctors are … I mean, patients aren't parents.'

'Really?' Dorothy was laughing openly at him. 'What gives you that idea?'

He was beginning to get extremely ratty. 'I mean, not *as such*. Anyway as a matter of fact I think letting people choose their doctors is a very bad idea. Very messy. Much tidier to allocate people to GPs. Much fairer. We could even cut the numbers in each doctor's practice, and everyone would stand an equal chance of getting the bad doctors.'

I was quietly amazed at Humphrey's – and the Civil Service's – concept of 'fair'.

Humphrey was now in full flow, passionate, emotional, scathing, committed like I have never seen. 'But we're not discussing the Health Service, Prime Minister, we're discussing education. And with respect, Prime Minister, I think you should know that the DES[2] will react with some caution to this rather novel proposal.'

This was the language of war! Humphrey had all guns blazing. I've never heard such abusive language from him.

I stayed calm. 'So you think they'll block it?'

'I mean,' he said, tight-lipped and angry, 'that they will give it the most serious and urgent consideration, but will insist on a thorough and rigorous examination of all the proposals, allied to a detailed feasibility study and budget analysis before producing a

---

2   The DES was the abbreviation for the then government Department of Education and Science.

consultative document for consideration by all interested bodies and seeking comments and recommendations to be incorporated in a brief for a series of working parties who will produce individual studies that will form the background for a more wide-ranging document considering whether or not the proposal should be taken forward to the next stage.'

He meant they'd block it! But it will be no problem. No problem at all. Because, as I told him, I have a solution to that. 'So I'll abolish the DES!' I mentioned casually.

He thought he'd misheard. 'I'm sorry?'

'We'll abolish it,' I repeated obligingly.

'Abolish it?' He couldn't grasp the meaning of the words.

'Why not?' Dorothy wanted to see if there were any reasons.

'Why not?' he said, his voice rising to the pitch of a Basil Fawlty at the end of his tether. 'Abolish Education and Science? It would be the end of civilisation as we know it.'

I shook my head at him. He was quite hysterical. 'No, we'd only be abolishing the department. Education and science will flourish.'

'Without a government department?' He was staring at us in horror, as though we were certifiably insane. 'Impossible!'

Dorothy seemed almost sorry for him. She tried to explain. 'Humphrey, government departments are tombstones. The Department of Industry marks the grave of industry. The Department of Employment marks the grave of employment. The Department of the Environment marks the grave of the environment. And the Department of Education marks where the corpse of British education is buried.'

He was staring the Goths and the Vandals in the face. He had no reply. So I asked him why we need the DES. What does it do? What's its role?

He tried to calm down and explain. 'I ... I hardly know where to begin,' he began. 'It lays down guidelines, it centralises and channels money to the Local Education Authorities and the University Grants Committee. It sets standards.'

I asked him a string of questions. 'Does it lay down the curriculum?'

'No, but ...'

'Does it select and change head teachers?'

'No, but ...'

'Does it maintain school buildings?'

'No, but ...'

'Does it set and mark exams?'

'No, but ...'

'Does it select the children?'

'No, but ...'

'Then how,' I wanted to know, 'does the Secretary of State affect how *my* child does at *her* school?'

To Humphrey the answer was obvious. 'He supplies sixty per cent of the cash!'

So that's it. We were right. Dorothy pursued the cross-examination. 'Why can't the cash go straight from the Treasury to the schools? And straight to the University Grants Committee? Do we really need two thousand civil servants simply to funnel money from A to B?'

Almost in despair, he shook his head and cried: 'The DES also creates a legislative framework for education.'

What did he mean? There's hardly any legislation at all. What there is, the Department of the Environment could do – Environment deals with other local government matters.

Humphrey was fighting a desperate rearguard action. 'Prime

Minister, you *can't* be serious. Who would assess forward planning and staffing variations, variations in pupil population, the density of schooling required in urban and rural areas ... Who would make sure everything *ran properly?*'

'It doesn't run properly now,' I pointed out. 'Let's see if we can do better without the bureaucracy.'

'But who would plan for the future?'

I laughed. But I didn't just laugh, I laughed uproariously. Laughter overwhelmed me, for the first time since I'd been Prime Minister. Tears were rolling down my cheeks. 'Do you mean?' I finally gasped, breathless, weeping with laughter, 'that education in Britain today is what the Department of Education *planned?*'

'Yes, of course,' said Humphrey, and then went immediately and without hesitation straight into reverse. 'No, certainly not.'

Dorothy was getting bored with the meeting. She stood up. 'Two thousand five hundred private schools seem to solve these planning problems every day,' she commented curtly. 'They just respond to changing circumstances, supply and demand. Easy.'

I wanted to give Humphrey one last chance. 'Is there anything else the DES does?'

His eyes whizzed back and forth, as he thought furiously. 'Um ... er ... um.'

I stood up too. 'Fine,' I said. 'That's it. We don't need it, do we? *Quod erat demonstrandum.*'

ABOUT THE IEA

The Institute is a research and educational charity (No. CC 235 351), limited by guarantee. Its mission is to improve understanding of the fundamental institutions of a free society with particular reference to the role of markets in solving economic and social problems.

The IEA achieves its mission by:

- a high-quality publishing programme
- conferences, seminars, lectures and other events
- outreach to school and college students
- brokering media introductions and appearances

The IEA, which was established in 1955 by the late Sir Antony Fisher, is an educational charity, not a political organisation. It is independent of any political party or group and does not carry on activities intended to affect support for any political party or candidate in any election or referendum, or at any other time. It is financed by sales of publications, conference fees and voluntary donations.

In addition to its main series of publications the IEA also publishes a quarterly journal, *Economic Affairs*, and has two specialist programmes – Environment and Technology, and Education.

The IEA is aided in its work by a distinguished international Academic Advisory Council and an eminent panel of Honorary Fellows. Together with other academics, they review prospective IEA publications, their comments being passed on anonymously to authors. All IEA papers are therefore subject to the same rigorous independent refereeing process as used by leading academic journals.

IEA publications enjoy widespread classroom use and course adoptions in schools and universities. They are also sold throughout the world and often translated/reprinted.

Since 1974 the IEA has helped to create a world-wide network of 100 similar institutions in over 70 countries. They are all independent but share the IEA's mission.

Views expressed in the IEA's publications are those of the authors, not those of the Institute (which has no corporate view), its Managing Trustees, Academic Advisory Council members or senior staff.

Members of the Institute's Academic Advisory Council, Honorary Fellows, Trustees and Staff are listed on the following page.

The Institute gratefully acknowledges financial support for its publications programme and other work from a generous benefaction by the late Alec and Beryl Warren.

200

Other papers recently published by the IEA include:

WHO, What and Why?
Transnational Government, Legitimacy and the World Health Organization
Roger Scruton
Occasional Paper 113; ISBN 0 255 36487 3
£8.00

The World Turned Rightside Up
A New Trading Agenda for the Age of Globalisation
John C. Hulsman
Occasional Paper 114; ISBN 0 255 36495 4
£8.00

The Representation of Business in English Literature
Introduced and edited by Arthur Pollard
Readings 53; ISBN 0 255 36491 1
£12.00

Anti-Liberalism 2000
The Rise of New Millennium Collectivism
David Henderson
Occasional Paper 115; ISBN 0 255 36497 0
£7.50

The Changing Fortunes of Economic Liberalism

Yesterday, Today and Tomorrow
David Henderson
Occasional Paper 105 (new edition); ISBN 0 255 36520 9
£12.50

The Global Education Industry

Lessons from Private Education in Developing Countries
James Tooley
Hobart Paper 141 (new edition); ISBN 0 255 36503 9
£12.50

Saving Our Streams

The Role of the Anglers' Conservation Association in
Protecting English and Welsh Rivers
Roger Bate
Research Monograph 53; ISBN 0 255 36494 6
£10.00

Better Off Out?

The Benefits or Costs of EU Membership
Brian Hindley & Martin Howe
Occasional Paper 99 (new edition); ISBN 0 255 36502 0
£10.00

Buckingham at 25

Freeing the Universities from State Control
Edited by James Tooley
Readings 55; ISBN 0 255 36512 8
£15.00

Lectures on Regulatory and Competition Policy

Irwin M. Stelzer
Occasional Paper 120; ISBN 0 255 36511 X
£12.50

Misguided Virtue

False Notions of Corporate Social Responsibility
David Henderson
Hobart Paper 142; ISBN 0 255 36510 1
£12.50

HIV and Aids in Schools

The Political Economy of Pressure Groups and Miseducation
Barrie Craven, Pauline Dixon, Gordon Stewart & James Tooley
Occasional Paper 121; ISBN 0 255 36522 5
£10.00

The Road to Serfdom

The Reader's Digest *condensed version*
Friedrich A. Hayek
Occasional Paper 122; ISBN 0 255 36530 6
£7.50

Bastiat's *The Law*

Introduction by Norman Barry
Occasional Paper 123; ISBN 0 255 36509 8
£7.50

A Globalist Manifesto for Public Policy

Charles Calomiris
Occasional Paper 124; ISBN 0 255 36525 X
£7.50

Euthanasia for Death Duties

Putting Inheritance Tax Out of Its Misery
Barry Bracewell-Milnes
Research Monograph 54; ISBN 0 255 36513 6
£10.00

Liberating the Land

The Case for Private Land-use Planning
Mark Pennington
Hobart Paper 143; ISBN 0 255 36508 x
£10.00

IEA Yearbook of Government Performance 2002/ 2003

Edited by Peter Warburton
Yearbook 1; ISBN 0 255 36532 2
£15.00

Britain's Relative Economic Performance, 1870– 1999

Nicholas Crafts
Research Monograph 55; ISBN 0 255 36524 1
£10.00

Should We Have Faith in Central Banks?

Otmar Issing
Occasional Paper 125; ISBN 0 255 36528 4
£7.50

The Dilemma of Democracy

Arthur Seldon
Hobart Paper 136 (reissue); ISBN 0 255 36536 5
£10.00

Capital Controls: a 'Cure' Worse Than the Problem?

Forrest Capie
Research Monograph 56; ISBN 0 255 36506 3
£10.00

The Poverty of 'Development Economics'

Deepak Lal
Hobart Paper 144 (reissue); ISBN 0 255 36519 5
£15.00

Should Britain Join the Euro?

The Chancellor's Five Tests Examined
Patrick Minford
Occasional Paper 126; ISBN 0 255 36527 6
£7.50

Post-Communist Transition: Some Lessons

Leszek Balcerowicz
Occasional Paper 127; ISBN 0 255 36533 0
£7.50

A Tribute to Peter Bauer

John Blundell et al.

Occasional Paper 128; ISBN 0 255 36531 4

£10.00

Employment Tribunals

Their Growth and the Case for Radical Reform

J. R. Shackleton

Hobart Paper 145; ISBN 0 255 36515 2

£10.00

Fifty Economic Fallacies Exposed

Geoffrey E. Wood

Occasional Paper 129; ISBN 0 255 36518 7

£12.50

A Market in Airport Slots

Keith Boyfield (editor), David Starkie, Tom Bass & Barry Humphreys

Readings 56; ISBN 0 255 36505 5

£10.00

Money, Inflation and the Constitutional Position of the Central Bank

Milton Friedman & Charles A. E. Goodhart

Readings 57; ISBN 0 255 36538 1

£10.00

Railway.com

Parallels between the early British railways and the ICT revolution
Robert C. B. Miller
Research Monograph 57; ISBN 0 255 36534 9
£12.50

The Regulation of Financial Markets

Edited by Philip Booth & David Currie
Readings 58; ISBN 0 255 36551 9
£12.50

Climate Alarmism Reconsidered

Robert L. Bradley Jr
Hobart Paper 146; ISBN 0 255 36541 1
£12.50

To order copies of currently available IEA papers, or to enquire about availability, please contact:

Lavis Marketing
IEA orders
FREEPOST LON21280
Oxford OX3 7BR

Tel: 01865 767575
Fax: 01865 750079
Email: orders@lavismarketing.co.uk

The IEA also offers a subscription service to its publications. For a single annual payment, currently £40.00 in the UK, you will receive every title the IEA publishes across the course of a year, invitations to events, and discounts on our extensive back catalogue. For more information, please contact:

Subscriptions
The Institute of Economic Affairs
2 Lord North Street
London SW1P 3LB

Tel: 020 7799 8900
Fax: 020 7799 2137
Website: www.iea.org.uk